PLEASE DIE

I WANT A PROMOTION

HOW TO MAXIMIZE EMPLOYEE FLEXIBILITY AND CONTRIBUTION

by RICHARD ALLISON

MATRIX SYSTEMS INC.
P.O. BOX 1510
CHERAW, SOUTH CAROLINA
29520

Copyright (c) 1996 by Richard Allison

All rights reserved. No part of this book may be reproduced or transmitted in any form by any means, electronic or mechanical, including photo copying, recording or by any information storage and retrieval system, without permission in writing from the publisher.

Published by: Matrix Systems Incorporated
P.O. Box 1510
Cheraw, South Carolina
29520

Library of Congress Catalog Card Number: 96-96140

ISBN 1-57502-139-0

Cover Design by Crystal Knight

Please Die I Want a Promotion - may be ordered using the order form in the back of the book.

Printed in the USA by

Morris Publishing
3212 E. Hwy 30
Kearney, NE 68847
800-650-7888

Contents

Introduction

Part 1

Why Your Company Needs a High Performance Work Structure

Chapter 1
The Challenge — Page 1

Chapter 2
Inside the Traditional Work Structure — Page 12

Chapter 3
A Better Way — Page 25

Part 2

Moving to High Performance - Who does it?

Chapter 4
Building Corporate Support — Page 42

Chapter 5
Building your Design Team — Page 61

Chapter 6
Design Considerations for a New Site — Page 73

Part 3

High Performance - How it gets done.

Chapter 7 Getting Started	Page 82
Chapter 8 Calibration and Skill Set Building	Page 92
Chapter 9 Structuring Levels for Departments and Teams	Page 117

Part 4

Making the Transition to High Performance

Chapter 10 From Old to New Making the Transition	Page 158
Chapter 11 Training and Career Pathing for the New System	Page 169
Summary	Page 195
Glossary	Page 196
Index	Page 199
Appendix	Page 202
Suggested Reading	Page 204

Please Die - I Want A Promotion

"is an excellent insight into the kind of thinking that needs to take place to create the work systems of the future, systems that will effectively compete in a fast moving global marketplace."

John L. Sipple, President
The Business Resource Network Inc.

Dedicated to my family

Karen Sue
Charity Lynn
James Richard

Introduction

Organizations are made up of people that are looking for ways to contribute based on the values expressed in your pay and progression system. In most traditional systems, the overwhelming criteria is "time". Because of this, people in most industrial organizations simply mark time until someone dies, retires or quits. This book will show you how to develop a system that will reflect the real values of your organization like:

Technical Knowledge
Flexibility
Individual Determination
Overall Contribution

It will allow you to pay the top performers in your organization based on the values you design into your "High Performance Work Structure".

By recognizing the differences in people and their determination, your organization will unleash a powerful competitive advantage.

This structure applies equally as well to virtually any industry, that employs people to do operational and/or maintenance tasks. Industries such as: Paper, Textiles, Chemical, Food and Beverage, Plastics, Wood Products and others.

I have had the opportunity to work with several different industries and have yet to find where the principles presented in this book did not apply.

Richard Allison

Acknowledgements

I would like to thank the technicians, who by their actions prove every day that "High Performance Work Structures" unleash hidden potential.

Please Die - I Want A Promotion

Part 1

Why Your Company Needs A High Performance Work Structure

Chapter 1

The Challenge

In this book you will read about performance, about motivation, and above all about challenge. One of the driving forces in my life has been to find and develop better ways that *challenge* people to contribute. There is a personal reason for this: I have lived and worked with the frustration experienced by most technicians in the work place.

In 1974, after getting out of the Army, I felt lucky to get a job with a pulp and paper mill owned by a major corporation. For the next two and a half years, I sat on the assembly line. I had learned that an employee in my position normally spent two and one-half to three years waiting for the opportunity to bid on the next job classification. Depending on where you were in the bidding ladder, this movement rate could range from two and one-half to ten years. The average time spent waiting for an opening in the maintenance area, for example, was seven years.

As was (and still is) typical of American industry at the time, the promotion practices of this company were based on time and the opening of a vacancy which occurred when someone else quit, died, or retired. My fellow workers quickly indoctrinated me into this concept. My best chance for success was simply to "hang in there" for a long time. It's simple, Richard, they told me — just keep your mouth shut, do your job, and wait. So I did. I waited and I wondered — why didn't something happen? I would look at my fellow workers a few feet down the assembly line and wonder: When are they going to quit, retire, or die? There was nothing personal in my attitude; these were my only options for advancement. I had to wait for an opening in the system so I could get a twenty-five-cent raise in my hourly rate. I learned that as you moved up the job ladder, the jobs got less physical — though not necessarily more mental — and had more desirable qualities. Maybe that was why our contract negotiations spelled out dozens of different pay rates. I wondered what my education was doing to help me get ahead with this company. I talked to my fellow workers about family, hobbies, or leisure activities, but the subject of career growth, or ambition, or even simple *movement* never came up — unless the bid sheet was out for another job classification. I couldn't help thinking that I might excel in certain jobs, but no one ever asked me to show what I could do. No one wanted to hear about new ideas such as how to do some part of the production process more effectively.

I know I was not the only employee to have these thoughts. I could see it in the eyes of the new hires. But they would soon learn the score: everyone is the same here. We must make management treat us *"the same"* or they will treat us unfairly.

Perhaps I didn't understand the rules of the game. I got to thinking about why management would want to create this pay structure that kept employees de-motivated, frustrated, and locked into positions that didn't use their capabilities. The only reason I could come up with was that it was the simplest way to do it — or, at least, it was *familiar*. But the more I thought about it, the more frustrated I became. I wanted to do better, not only for the company, but also for my own sense of self-worth.

The funny thing was, we all knew there were certain people in the company you could count on to know their jobs extremely well. They took pride in whatever they were doing. Many times the managers knew it as well, but the system did not allow managers to promote these employees or otherwise reward them.

I waited out my time, and gradually I moved up to the higher-paying jobs, one step at a time. Eventually I got into a position I liked because of the pay as well as the particular work I was doing. All on-the-job training and experience previously received went out the window; I would never have to do those jobs again. The skills I had learned were gone. Sure, I still knew how to perform those other jobs, but after all the time I spent "in the barrel" I'd be out of my mind to want to do them again.

My story is not unique. If it were, there would probably be no reason to write on this subject. But the frustrations of workers and technicians everywhere are telling management to wake up: *Look at the potential you are wasting!*

This book describes a system for structuring jobs and promotional patterns that give people a *challenge*. Developing this system in a company is not easy; still, as trying as it may be to make the transition I'm about to describe, I have never heard a worker say they would like to go back to the old way. The possible exceptions are those "retired on the job" employees who liked the old system because they did not have to give anything beyond the minimum needed to get by from one day to the next.

Some people perceive challenge as *stress*. For example, the stress of preparing for a math exam in college, or the physical stress of getting into shape. What the old system produces, through absence of challenge or stress, is *distress*. Distress is being put into a situation where you feel stuck, with no possibility of change for the better. You have no control over your ability to advance, or the possibility of advancement is simply not there. You feel trapped in a system that doesn't value your contribution. That is *distress,* and it's a killer. Employees, workers, technicians — whatever title they go by, are all *people*. And individual people need challenges in order to grow. People improve by having to do: having to do a new thing; having to learn; having to demonstrate their ability.

If this does not occur, then people become stagnant. When people get stagnant, they wonder why they are in the position they are in, and they look for a way out. Keep the possibility of movement in front of the employees in your organization. Make it so *they* can determine how far they will go.

What's wrong with tradition

An old saying has it, "You get what you pay for." In the work place, that could just as easily be stated, *"You get what you ask for."* Industry has made great strides in technology, and that technology has greatly enhanced productivity. But for over 40 years, the pattern of progression from one industrial job to another has remained basically the same. Is that because it is the most efficient way to handle this movement? Is it because the capabilities of employees have not changed in 40 years? Or could it be that managers are most comfortable with tradition?

In fact, employees' capabilities *have* changed over the last 40 years. There *are* more efficient ways to handle progression. It may be less comfortable, at first, to manage in a way that promotes individual responsibility and capability, but if you do not address this issue — whether you are traditional or non-traditional — then time will address it for you.

Managers as well as employees must be challenged to develop a better product, to be highly productive, and to use their skills to highest level of capability. For the most part, industrial employees have possessed many desirable attributes all along; we as managers just did not ask or expect workers to demonstrate them. Industrial employees often have the following attributes:

° They are well educated.
° They can be motivated.
° They will be with us over the long term.
° They are more flexible than machines.
° They want to contribute.
° They react to their environment.
° They take pride in a job well done.
° They are important to your long-term success.

Since these attributes exist among our human resources, what have we done to make better use of them? Many of us have established a team environment to help us find ways to more effectively run our companies. This has led to positive gains, and should be an integral part of business.

But it is not enough. We need to consider the basic structure of the progression pattern in order to change the perception of how individuals succeed in the work force. If, as an employee, I have the perception that all I need to do is to wait my turn for the next job classification and let time take care of the opportunity, then I will have no incentive to do anything but wait. On the other hand, if it is my responsibility to pursue whatever career opportunities are available, then the level of success I achieve will be more directly related to what I am willing and able to contribute. Typically in traditional systems, a new employee is assigned to an entry level crew and, over time, moves to some increasing level of responsibility. In this type of progression, movement depends on *somebody else* quitting, retiring, or dying — and may have little to do with the attributes or skills of the employee anticipating the move. Over the years, management has conditioned employees to believe that this is the best method for everyone concerned. In the traditional progression pattern, employees seek movement because the higher classified jobs are perceived to be easier, better paid, and sometimes more satisfying. Those reasons will be present for employees in any system. The difference between a traditional and a high performance work structure is that employees in the latter have greater control over their own progression through increasing levels of skills, responsibilities, and pay. Employees are rewarded based on what they are willing and able to give, and management gets what it asks for.

One feature of the traditional system that I really do not understand is why a company would go through the effort of training an employee for some particular task, and then abandon that training the next time the person moves. Are we not a combination of all the things we have learned and the experiences that we gain? Let's find a way to take advantage of the whole person and their abilities, and at the same time allow that person to be recognized for the qualities that make the individual unique to the organization.

Management has an obligation to provide a work structure that allows employees to contribute based on their ability. A properly designed, high performance work structure that allows people to progress based on ability and willingness to contribute, will unleash your organization from an also-ran to become the leader of the pack. The system that I am going to describe to you does not imply that I think every individual will be a better contributor. It does, however, offer the opportunity to obtain more from people who have the desire and ability to contribute more. It simply gives your people a reason to contribute to their potential. It will affect the vast majority of your organization in a positive way, if the design is correctly structured.

Employee Attributes

We've used the terms "willing" and "able" to describe the kind of employees who shine under a high performance work structure. Let's look at these terms in greater detail. There are four basic categories of employees in industry. We have employees that are:

- ° Able and willing to do
- ° Able but unwilling to do
- ° Willing but unable to do
- ° Unwilling and unable to do

Why do different people fall into these four categories? Starting with the "unwilling and unable." This individual is a "poor fit" — obviously unsuited for your organization and perhaps for any organization. The presence of more than one or two of these individuals in your company indicates that you may want to evaluate the way you screen the people you hire. You are going to expend needed energy to eliminate this person from your organization — energy which could have been spent on developing a person that is better suited for your business. It was a mistake from the start on the employee's part, and on yours, due to some flaw in your screening process. Will this happen? Probably! We are, after all, human.

The next category is the person who is "willing but unable." There are normally two main reasons this person is having difficulty being productive. The first concern is the job classification does not suit the individual. Some individuals may be suited more for production work, while others find their niche in maintenance. The second most common reason for this occurrence is that the employee has not received the training needed to succeed in a particular job. The organization should review its training program. Since the employee is willing, with improved training and guidance there should be a way to enable that person to contribute to the organization.

The next and largest category — and the one that industry itself has created — is "able but unwilling." These individuals are intelligent and they understand the promotion pattern. They realize that they have no real reason to strive for a higher employment level because time is the controlling factor that determines success in the organization. These employees know that contribution to the organization does not necessarily lead to individual success. Thus, employees in traditional systems simply mark time until they can attain that specific job classification that yields some degree of personal satisfaction. There is a tremendous amount of potential among these individuals in your organization. Are you willing to change to a structure that increases the perception of personal as well as organizational success?

The last category is the category that all organizations want: those who are "willing and able" to contribute to the success of the company, knowing that by doing so they will become personally successful as well. The new employees that you bring into your organization are generally in this category when you hire them. Does your system keep them there?

When you hire an individual, that person is almost always in the "willing and able" mode. What typically occurs, however, is that after a few weeks or months the individual suddenly comes to the realization that it really is just a job. The person feels trapped, with no way to move based on their own willingness, and gradually moves into the "able but unwilling" category.

Some of the more progressive organizations have determined that people really do make a difference if the structure allows it. As you consider the move toward a high performance work structure, know that pitfalls and opportunities await your organization. This book is designed to assist your company in the decisions, design, and implementation of the new system. Our employees expect management to set the tone for what contribution means in industry. If that means accepting the minimum, then *"we get what we ask for."* On the other hand, if we challenge our employees to use all of their capabilities, then survival in today's business environment is assured.

Chapter 2

Inside the Traditional Work Structure

Let's look at an all-too-typical example of how employees use the values of the organization to set their work goals. When I first met Bob C., he had been working at a paper plant in the South for about 15 years. His progression at the plant was as follows:

Yard crew	2 years
Wrapline helper	3 years
Winder helper	5 years
Backstand helper	5 years

Bob's movement from one job classification to another was based solely on putting in the typical amount of time in each position. His chance to move depended on someone dying, retiring or quitting. The question of what the specific jobs entailed was unimportant, as all plants have different classifications. If we look a little deeper into Bob's progression, it will reveal the real story of his motivation within the company. In this traditional movement pattern, Bob could have taken any of a number of different jobs. As he put in his time with the company, Bob balanced the amount of money he would earn against the amount of mental and physical effort that the position required. The job of backstand helper required Bob to work 15 minutes out of each hour; the rest of the time he basically sat in the break area.

What was Bob doing with all those hours he spent in the break area? Selling fish! This was a second job he ran as a home business, and he used the extra time in the break room to process orders, complete his bookkeeping, and so forth.

Bob is not a bad guy; he simply had determined where he could get the most value for his time with the company. For his part, he was a very successful person. He worked within the value system that had been established by his company's promotion structure. Everyone knew that Bob was a smart person and could, if he wanted to, operate the more complex equipment and systems. But the company gave him no reason to do so.

There is a happy ending to this story. Bob's company made the transition to a high performance work structure.

As a result, it became obvious that employees were valued for their contributions because their efforts were reflected in their pay rates. Bob now shows his ability by preforming the jobs he previously learned and now he also works as lead operator for the cutter layboy and the winder. The company is using all of Bob's capabilities, and Bob is earning a higher income at his primary job. The outcome is that they are both winners. Would Bob have preferred his company to retain the old system? That is always a possibility, but over the long run Bob will find more encouragement to stay with the company because the plant is making better use of his talents. Remember, the organizational system that your company uses sets the value system for the employees.

Fairness versus Equality

For more than 40 years, management direction concerning promotion patterns has been to treat people equally — or "the same" — as much as possible. In practice, the terms "equal" or "the same" are misleading. *What this concept really means is that employees are promoted based on one common denominator — time — without regard for skills, abilities, talents, interests, or contributions to the company.*

This practice has stifled the motivation of employees to contribute to the best of their ability. The fact is, Americans by nature are a competitive group of individuals. We struggle not to be equal. We strive to be a better athlete or better in one thing or another. Since traditional systems promote the illusion of equality even though we are not equal, they ignore the normal competitive nature of each individual.

People are *not equal* in:

° Education
° Experience
° Willingness to actively participate
° Willingness to learn
° Motivation/ambition

To treat all people "the same" in your organization is to limit their ability to contribute.

Flexibility or Stagnation

Be prepared to look at typical job tasks from a different perspective. Traditional job classifications only look at three criteria: What is the smallest safe operation a person can do that is productive? Second, how do the various tasks rank on a scale of least desirable to most desirable? Third let's make sure the job task area won't tax the newest employee's brain. After all, these people are willing and able to do what ever the company wants, but we need to change that as soon as possible. Sorry, couldn't help myself, lets get back on track. The individuals at the bottom of the ladder in a traditional pay and promotion system perform the least desirable tasks until vacancies are created, through death, retirement or quitting, at the higher pay levels.

Now the company needs an employee to take an experienced employees place that has died, retired or quit. The company moves each employee in turn into the next position. Then hire a new employee for the bottom position. By this time the entire organization has been turned upside down in what becomes a domino effect. The ripple goes through the entire organization, and that ripple turns into a wave of filling each job in turn with somebody new and less experienced in each task area. Experience has shown that this ripple effect actually lasts about a year from the time the first vacancy was created until all of the task areas are filled. Then it can start all over again with another vacancy. The result is that the different departments are in a constant state of flux because of employee turnover. This is a major issue when you relate it to productivity. For example, let's say your company has six moves that occur because of one vacancy. What is the possibility you will get the best person in each of the six positions? As an educated estimate, if you got more than 50 percent of the positions filled by the best workers, that would be very good. Am I saying that your people are not trying or would not eventually learn the task and perform it adequately? No! I am saying there is a better method for filling vacancies, one that treats people fairly and gives the business a break from this ripple effect that is so disruptive.

People will respond to an opportunity for promotion for only a few reasons: more money, easier job, greater job satisfaction, peer recognition and management recognition. These reasons are the same in any system. The system you design must break the domino effect. It must encourage the distribution of unpleasant as well as desirable task areas, not because we want to treat people equally, but because we need a system that allows people equal opportunity for advancement.

Maintenance Skills in Traditional Organizations

In most traditional structures, there are normally three divisions of skills on site: operations, mechanical maintenance, and electrical/instrumentation maintenance. In some ways mechanical maintenance has already made a move toward a high performance work structure, because of the advancement toward the multi-craft concept that is currently very popular in industry. However, we still have a lot of industries using craft lines. In order to understand the high performance work structure, we must first take a closer look at the existing situations in industry. First let's examine the craft line system.

Craft System:

- Welder
- Pipefitter
- Millwright
- Rigger
- Iron Worker
- Painter
- Carpenter
- Lubrication

There are, of course, more craft lines than those listed. One of the major problems with the craft line system is that it is *economically irresponsible to pay three people to do a task that one person could do.*

For example, let's look at a pump installation project. In a craft line situation you would have to call three different craft people to install the pump: a Rigger, a Millwright, and a Pipefitter. Not only do these three people have to come to the job site, but the sequence of events would also have to be timed so that each one could do their specific task in the proper order. It takes more time and more people.

Now in many organizations mechanical maintenance has gone to a multi-craft concept. Under this structure, one person might have all three skills needed for the pump installation project. This multi-skilled person would thus complete the job with less personnel and in less time. For you non-believers, this shift was not done simply to make people work harder. It was to be more effective and efficient. Companies that price themselves out of business through over staffing and inefficient methods do not add to the job security of anyone. The cost, in the end, is job loss.

In multi-craft systems, people are expected to perform several different craft areas with proficiency. Over the years industry has proven this to be an effective way to develop more skills in the mechanical maintenance work force. So why change it with the structure I am advocating in this book?

The multi-craft system is a step in the right direction, but there must be greater emphasis on the value of skills. Most companies also need a better method of identifying what skills are required in specific departments. A method is needed that selects the person who is best suited for a particular skill area.

We have seen that the mechanical craft lines have gradually moved to a multi-craft system to gain efficiency. In the same manner, the systems that once split electrical skills into one craft and instrumentation into another are gradually becoming combined in many industries. From my perspective, the combining of electrical and instrumentation lines has met with greater resistance than the multi-craft system, and the move to combine them has been slower. Yet the benefits are the same.

So how do we get there from here? If your company is using the multi-craft system or combining electrical and instrumentation skills now, the change will not be nearly so big. If the system you're using is craft line, you should at least take the step to the multi-craft system. And then why not go all the way to the high performance work structure?

Training or Programming?

It never ceases to amaze me how management continues to underestimate the ability of American workers. Perhaps that is one reason why the traditional approach toward work structure has remained the same for so long. The traditional method is not threatening; it usually does not stretch people's capabilities; and it preserves the need for more managers and supervision. Think about people you know who were asked to do a special project, and they did a lot more than was expected. It happens that way more than the other! They were simply asked to do the job, given the direction and support necessary to accomplish the task, and they excelled.

In order for employees to excel at the variety of tasks

needed in industry, they need — in addition to direction and support — proper training. In a traditional business, determining eligibility for training is fairly simple. When a job vacancy occurs a person is selected to fill that vacancy and starts training. In contrast, a high performance work structure provides more opportunity for obtaining skills. This increased promotion potential occurs when a variety of skills are available to those employees who desire to stretch to the best of their ability.

Now let's review a distribution of skills in a traditional system. In most traditional systems in American industry a person will learn one, perhaps two specific job classifications: the one the person is getting paid for on a daily basis, and the one that person might occupy on a temporary basis if a vacancy occurs. In some cases an employee can refuse to move unless it is for a permanent change that they specifically want. This says, in effect, that the most I can expect an individual to attain in my organization is one or two specific job skills. There is one notable exception, and that is the designation of a utility position, in which an individual will be called upon to do several jobs depending on the need. But for the vast majority of employees, the typical job classification is limited to one or two specific tasks. Is that all that we can expect employees to be capable of doing? In a traditional system we will never know!

If we chart out the skill distribution in a traditional work crew, as shown in Exhibit A, you can see that the total number of skills available on the team or crew is easily determined. Compare this with Exhibit B, which diagrams the skill availability for a crew in a high performance work structure. As you can see, the number of skills on the same size crew more than doubles. It simply states that people are capable of doing several things well. Exhibit B is a normal distribution of skills that will occur if people are allowed to seek their own level of success. This normal bell curve distribution is not allowed to occur in a traditional work structure. After studying the pitfalls of the traditional work structure, it should be obvious that there is a better way. This process allows both employees and management to be winners. If the opportunity is there for the individual, then the opportunity is there for the company to make better use of that person's abilities. The key is to have a structure that allows the individual to determine their own level of achievement.

Your people are capable of contributing much more than they have ever been asked to perform. So let us proceed into the considerations you must look for when creating an effective high performance work structure.

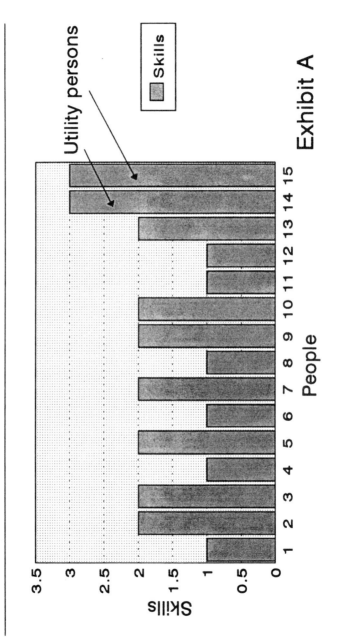

Non Traditional Distribution

Normal Distribution over 6 Levels

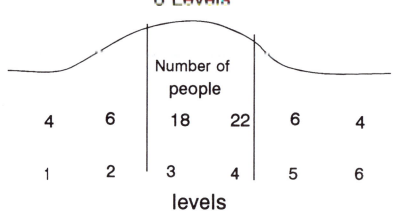

4	6	18	22	6	4
1	2	3	4	5	6

levels

Four 15 Person Teams

Number of people
 X
Each Level   =   Total skills available   212

A detailed explaination in part 3

"High Performance-How it gets done"

Exhibit B

Chapter 3

A Better Way

By now you may be thinking that a high performance work structure sounds like a good idea, but the task of converting to this new system seems overwhelming. Parts 2 and 3 of this book will take you step by step through the design and conversion process. But first let's look in greater detail at the components of high performance work structures. Reaching a goal is easier if you know where you're going!

One question frequently asked is, does the high performance concept apply to union as well as non-union plants? The answer is Yes! In Parts 2 and 3, I will discuss the slight variations that apply to union or non union plants as we go through the process. Another concern is, how does the design of a high performance work structure apply to new plants? The answer to that is that the process applies equally well to existing and new plants. The main difference is in who does what. Considerations for new plants will be discussed at the end of Part 2.

The Components of High Performance

As illustrated in Exhibit C, think of an *"umbrella"* that covers several different components of a high performance work structure. These components work together to produce a unified system for a company, or for an individual plant within the company. Let's briefly look at each of these components:

° **Calibration of Skills.** In this step, the design team reviews the individual skills that comprise each task the business requires, and assigns a point value to each.

° **Determining Skill Sets.** The design team decides how to combine individual skills into skill sets or modules. This will be used in determining pay levels.

° **Active Participation.** This involves leadership, interpersonal skills, and anything that goes beyond the basic task to enhance the organization's productivity. By building active participation into the design, a high performance work structure automatically rewards employees for exhibiting these qualities.

  ° **Pay Levels.** Once the skill sets have been developed to include both technical skills and active participation, the next task is to assign pay rates at each level.

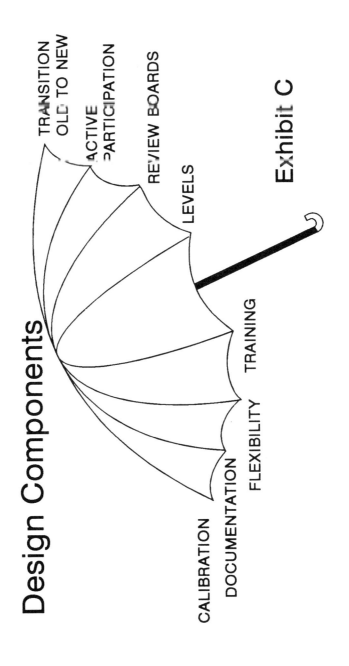

° **Training Requirements.** The company's resulting skill sets and pay levels may be unique to the organization. Now is the time to specify the training required for an employee to be certified in the various skill sets.

° **Review Boards.** In most cases, some testing process will be needed to determine which employees are eligible to work in the various skill sets. Establishing review boards is one way to accomplish this.

° **Documentation.** This is the overall concept of documenting an employee's qualifications to perform each skill set.

By breaking the process of developing a high performance work structure into these component parts, the task of accomplishing the conversion will be much easier. You'll notice I spoke of the "design team." In the system I'm about to describe, you will select several teams to do the tasks needed to design the structure and accomplish the conversion. Keep in mind the illustration of the umbrella, the design teams will follow the same idea. I'll discuss the selection and training of design team members in more detail in Part 2.

Promotion and Challenge

As I said earlier, there are a few basic reasons why employees seek promotion and job advancement. These reasons include more money, more satisfying work, and/or greater recognition, and will remain the same no matter how the work place is structured. A system that is structured so that these motivating factors are tied to the job itself will best encourage employees to contribute.

In a high performance work structure, pay is based on a person's contribution to the organization. This will be explained later in the discussions on skill sets and pay levels. What is important to the success of this concept is the distribution of skills, as determined by the calibration part of your design process.

The system you design will need to break the "domino effect" by distributing unpleasant as well as more rewarding tasks in a fair manner. Employees advance to higher pay levels by acquiring and demonstrating more skill sets, which will include basic as well as more advanced job skills. It will also be possible to combine some of the areas we have discussed previously, such as maintenance and operations skills. The idea is to take a broad look at all the tasks in the business, keeping in mind that each one must be considered in relationship to one another.

A major factor in an individual's success under the new system will be *timing*. Not *time,* as in the traditional system, but timing: making a skill set available when and where it is needed in the business. Individual employees can greatly enhance their effectiveness by preparing for the opportunities as they arise. This requires effective planning and communication between the individual and the company. As the saying goes, *Proper Prior Planning Prevents Piss Poor Performance.* This type of planning and communication is typically absent in traditional promotion systems. I will discuss employee career planning later in Part 4.

The overall umbrella of calibration, skill sets, pay levels, and review underlies a very important concept of the high performance work structure: *Employees can and should be responsible and accountable for the success they are "willing and able" to achieve in your organization.* This is what challenges employees to contribute. It is **not** a true statement for the traditional promotion pattern. It **is** the foundation of system design for the high performance work structure.

Many managers view team systems as places where accountability is given to the teams. This is necessary in many cases. However, the individual progression in a properly designed system should be up to the determination of the individual.

I do not want to give the wrong impression: I am an advocate of the team systems. The high performance structure works great with team systems; in fact, it makes plant teams more effective, especially for teams that deal with such areas as problem solving, technical issues, safety, cost, or reliability.

The structure of a high performance work system allows a team to function more naturally. In any team there are all kinds of abilities and individual variations. In a football team, like the San Francisco 49ers, each individual is paid based upon their contribution to the team. Imagine hearing that from now on the 49ers were going to promote a player based simply upon his time with the team. You would say that was crazy, and you would be right! Sport team owners and managers recognize the differences in players' abilities, and pay accordingly. This sounds natural enough, and the team members recognize it as appropriate. Differences actually make the team stronger, since the players know that what they contribute to the total effort will be rewarded in their pay. There is one problem with team systems: people seem to forget that teams are made up of individuals. You might define a team as a group of "unequal" individuals. That is really the strength of a team — the different strengths of its members, and the ability to recognize those differences. A true high performance work structure allows for synergism in a team and at the same time promotes individual contribution. This can be done, and it is the right thing to do.

In a traditional system you can look into the future easily, and simply wait for that domino effect to allow movement. Under a high performance system, the process of choosing skill sets will require employees to get involved in making good personal and business decisions that will affect their future. Managers will determine what skills are needed for the business to function as a world class operation, while allowing the department teams to determine who attains what particular skill set based on the criteria your design teams will establish.

When I visit various companies to help them design their work system, I often look around the work place and say to myself, this employee is going to rise above the rest or I hope that person makes it. I have found that at least 50 percent of the time I'm wrong. That is because a specific individual's level of determination and drive can not be predicted with any kind of accuracy. Remember, the system we are designing is for the person who is willing and able to do what is necessary to move the business and themselves along. So why not let the person's own self-determination be the controlling factor?

Fast Response in Today's Business Environment

We've talked about how high performance work structures benefit the employee by allowing greater opportunity for advancement, and by giving the employee some degree of control over his or her own progress. Now let's look at how these systems can benefit the business by increasing flexibility, performance, and responsiveness — all of which are needed to compete in today's business environment.

- **Skill sets are aligned to business needs.**

In a traditional system, the relationship of one job to another is often non-existent. When a vacancy occurs, the business suffers because a particular skill is lost until the person leaving is replaced. This problem ripples throughout the organization, as was previously discussed.

In contrast, by aligning the business needs with the skill sets available, movement in a high performance organization will increase the total number of skills available, not detract from it. Personnel movement can and should enhance the business's functioning, because each employee is able to contribute more overall, not just simply perform some different job.

- **All components of a skill set should be a shared responsibility.**

Is this strictly to share the more physical or unpleasant duties? On the surface that sounds reasonable and does have some merit. However, the most important reason for spreading the components of skill sets around is so that all employees in a department will have an overall understanding of that specific skill area. People who have a well-rounded understanding of the operation make better decisions, even if their individual work area for the night or for the week is small. If someone else is in trouble they can lend a hand. Well-rounded employees can help make a better work environment by suggesting changes or ideas for improvements.

◦ **Lines of progression become blurred.**

Why worry about blurring lines of progression? Because in this system you pay for overall contribution, not just for the job classification. This gives the business a chance to change the perception of what success is all about. An employee does not have to aim for one or two specific positions — for example, control room operator — to be successful. There can be 20 to 200 possible ways to progress to the same level. It's not about waiting in line, it's about the skills a company needs. It's about an individuals willingness to contribute.

◦ **Dozens of pay grades are reduced to just a few.**

This system is based on the idea of *Keep it Simple*, and your payroll department will love it. If you have a union organization, the skill set concept will make negotiation less complex. This is especially true when both the union and management will have participated in the calibration of the skill sets.

◦ **The one-job-one person syndrome is eliminated.**

People are simply capable of developing more skills than the traditional systems ask for. Will the perception of one-job-one-person be difficult to eliminate? Certainly; after all, industry has demanded this concept for years. Was it wrong all along? Maybe not at first, but now is the time for a change. The person in your organization who will least like the new system is the person who has the ability but not the willingness to give any more than the minimum to get by. Is that really the employee's fault? The old system told its employees how it defined success, and now you are trying to change the rules. However, you can do something about this issue when you give direction to your teams for making the transition from old to new. We will consider this in detail in Part 4.

◦ **Active participation is encouraged**

What defines active participation in your organization? In most traditional companies, it simply means doing your particular job exceptionally well. In a high performance work structure, active participation has nothing to do with actually performing a job function at a plant. Active participation is a combination of leadership (situational as well as general), exercising "soft" or interpersonal skills, and generally doing the things beyond the technical task that enhance the organization's productivity. Hiring an individual to just do a basic task is a waste of a person's capability. You must ask the individual to participate in the whole organization. The way you do this is by including participation in your promotion structure. If you ask for this activity outside of the promotion structure, you will get limited participation and the people who have the capability and are willing to give are not fairly rewarded in your organization. The role of active participation needs to be designed so that everyone in your organization can and is expected to participate at some level.

As an employee rises in your organization, it should be a natural occurrence that the degree of active participation expected and contributed becomes greater and greater. A guideline is necessary in order to measure active participation. It is important that the things that your organization expects its people to accomplish or participate in be a natural order of business.

But Does it Work?

The best proof of the value of a high performance work structure is success. It is natural, when presented with a new system, to wonder *"does it work?"* Chip Aiken, Plant Manager of Buckeye Cellulose (formerly Procter & Gamble Cellulose) thinks it does. His plant, which has over 850 employees and is a union site, made the change following company direction in 1986. Since that time, employees have been trained not only in the physical operation of their job, but also in the principles, the "whys," and the fundamental science behind their tasks. All of this results in employees with much higher skills. Flexibility has increased, as well. Employees are expected to maintain and utilize their different skills. This allows for a team plan to cover absences due to vacation, training, support projects, and so on.

Buckeye Cellulose is continuously evaluating its cost effectiveness as a result of this change. Aiken notes that as the capability of the organization improves, the business results improve. This opens up new opportunities for cost structure improvements. Says Aiken, "I believe our system of work is fundamental to our success. Without the creativity and mastery in our organization and the ability to respond quickly to business challenges, we would not be a successful manufacturing organization — we might not even be in business."

Asked what advice he would offer to companies beginning the shift to a high performance work structure, Aiken replied, "Get the people who will be affected by the change involved in designing the change." The next section will show you how to do just that.

Willamette Industries in Bennettsville, South Carolina is another example of a company that is seeing the benefits of utilizing a high performance work structure. This plant has approximately 300 employees and is non-union. It was a new start-up facility and hired all green employee's. This plant is highly automated and has been utilizing the high performance work structure since 1990. The other companies that have visited the plant have used such statements as "I can't believe the flexibility in your employee's". "The Knowledge base is amazing for a plant of six years"
This is an excellent example of a contribution based work structure.

John Sipple the president of:
" The Business Resource Network Inc"
says:

"The underlying principle to High Performance Work Systems boils down to this: are you a Theory x person or are you a Theory y person. Most American businesses are founded on Theory x beliefs - that people can't be trusted, are lazy and don't want to work. Because of that belief many controls and levels of management exist to keep workers working.

Some companies are learning a better way, the Theory y way. This is the belief that people do want to contribute and they recognize deep down that to be successful as individuals they must help their companies be successful. The companies that understand (and believe) this, are creating exciting new ways for their organizations to be successful - and the business results are fantastic!

In the future the successful companies will be the ones who learn to do this. Those still entrenched in Theory x thinking will die. It's really that simple."

Part 2

Moving to High Performance

Who does it?

Chapter 4

Building Corporate Support

Any company considering the change to a high performance work structure needs support and direction from the corporate level. Whether your business is a large corporation or a single plant, it is important that the top managers understand and support the concept, as well as provide direction on the outcome desired. The benefits and challenges that come with this type of conversion are many. Support from all levels of management is important to follow through when tough decisions are necessary.

This type of system is not a *social experiment*. It must be based on measurable business results that can be expected and delivered through the increased use of the employees' talents. Those talents, which for the most part has always been present. Those talents simply have not been asked for because of the traditional structure of your work system. Every plant, or production site has a work structure, and every work structure sends a message to its employees. Use the development of your system to send the right message.

The Corporate Management Role

Guidelines issued at the corporate level should be general and value oriented. An example of corporate guidelines that would be appropriate for developing the new work system is:

- *The system must be flexible*
- *Everyone must be encouraged to participate*
- *The system must value the contributor*
- *The changes must be economically justifiable*

There are many more values that a corporation may want to state as direction. However, be as general as possible to allow room for the plant and department design teams to develop their own unique high performance work structure. The corporate values that are stated in the overall direction will be handed to the teams that will put the fabric on the umbrella. The direction should be broad enough to allow the teams to be innovative when looking at alternatives to the structure. At the same time the direction should narrow down, pointing out the company's view of the correct path toward high performance.

An excellent way for corporate managers to gain a perspective on this process is to visit other companies, both within and outside your industry, that have been successful in implementing high performance work structures. Through these visits, you may identify certain characteristics that you may want to have your design teams employ.

Talk to the people in other companies who have actually designed high performance work systems. I have had the opportunity to work on system design in both new locations and retro-fitted plants, in union and non-union plants. As a result, I have been able to learn from others' mistakes and identify certain pitfalls as well as reasons to consider issues in some logical order.

One thing you can be sure of is that each plant needs as much pertinent information as possible. An evaluation of your plant by an outside source may be an option as the first step to provide the corporate or plant managers with some insight into how big a hurdle the conversion or the implementation may be. See the Appendix for information on locating and working with consultants.

It can be said that all work systems are perfectly designed to achieve the results they achieve, because it is the exact sum of the parts you put in the design. Your work system will be the sum total of the thought, understanding, and attention to detail with which you design into it. Still, it may not accomplish exactly what you intended if you have not researched and compiled the necessary information to give your company that extra jump start. Traditional work systems are giving the results that are in that particular design, but this is no longer a competitive way to continue in business. As important as it is to do a good job up front with your design, understand from the beginning that the process will need to be evaluated periodically to determine if it is meeting all your goals. Do not be so rigid that you think the original design of any work structure is untouchable! Make sure the high performance work structure works for you, and if necessary make the appropriate changes for success. But with good up-front design, your structure will normally require only minor adjustments in the future.

Before we move on, allow me to give you a piece of philosophy that will help with whatever your organization decides to do about work structure: "*You often do not get what you expect, but you almost always get what you inspect.*" If you inspect for results, you will at least have the opportunity to correct the structure if it doesn't meet your expectations.

Plant Management

The management of each specific plant within the company has the task of interpreting the general value statements from the corporate level. This is accomplished by sharing with the employees the reasons for the change, and by communicating what the corporate level expects accomplished with the move to a high performance work structure. At this level, management's task is to develop the plant design team a road map to guide them on their journey. This map should furnish the design team enough guidance so that the team members do not spend too much time on design elements that are already decided, thus running up against the wall called "management decision."

Plant management, by narrowing the scope of work for the design team, really is setting out the essential elements of the work structure for the plant. The direction from plant management must give the design team enough flexibility so they have an opportunity to develop innovative answers. Furthermore, the plant's direction should follow logically from the corporate guidelines so that the design team will be able to take the next step and have the plant design process follow naturally. I suggest you give some title to these directions to the plant design team, such as "Plant Design Principles" or "Plant Design Elements." You should also request constant evaluations of the design as it is in progress, so that you can see if the design team is meeting the parameters.

On another note, do not be concerned if the plant management's design elements are occasionally challenged. The plant design process will sometimes take an unexpected turn and make the plant's managers look again at how they interpreted the corporate level direction. The plant design team, as we will see, is made up of a synergistic compliment of employees, and they may generate some alternatives that upper management had not considered. However, if you did your homework, the challenges will be few and your flexibility will be noticed.

Here are some potential design elements at the plant management level:

- *The design will treat people fairly, not necessarily equally.*
- *The design will value differences.*
- *Employees will show flexibility by demonstration of more than one skill area.*
- *Employees will be paid based on their overall contribution.*
- *Active Participation will be a part of the promotion process.*
- *Decisions will be made at the lowest logical level in the organization.*

Please Die - I Want A Promotion

- *Opportunity for advancement will reflect business needs.*
- *Knowledge without utilization of skills will not be valued.*
- *Communication skills will be valued.*
- *Pay reviews will include peers.*
- *Team composition will balance skills.*
- *Pay levels* will be "relatively equal."*
- *Training documentation will support the promotion procedure.*
- *Performance evaluations will occur at least once a year.*
- *Time on the job will not be the over riding element that determines success.*

---

*To be discussed in Part 3.

Again, these are examples. Certainly some of the directions to your design team will be different, according to your values. This does not make them wrong. Remember, your system will work perfectly, but whether it works in the way you originally envisioned will depend on the actual message that is being sent by the structure you employ.

Before we proceed any further into the design elements, let's align these fifteen plant management design elements with the corporate direction to make sure we have given the plant design team direction on each of the corporate elements:

Corporate Value: System must be flexible

Plant direction:
- Employees will show flexibility by demonstration of more than one skill area.
- Employees will be paid based on their overall contribution.

Corporate Value: Participation an expectation.

Plant direction:
- Active participation will be a part of the promotion process.
- Decisions will be made at the lowest logical level.
- Performance evaluations will occur at least once a year.
- The design will value differences.

Corporate Direction: System must value the contributor.

Plant direction:
- Employees will be paid based on their overall contribution.
- Knowledge without utilization of skills will not be valued.
- Communication skills will be valued.

° Time on the job will not be the overriding element that dictates success.
° Training documentation will support the promotion process.

Corporate Direction: System must be economically practical.

Plant direction:
° Opportunity for advancement will be based on business needs.
° Pay reviews will include peers.
° Teams will balance skills.

Now you have put the process on the road to success by giving the design team enough direction to focus them on the target, but with sufficient flexibility to design a system that will allow ownership by the plant's employees. One element that is of critical importance to the individual employee is the opportunity to affect the day-to-day results of the work place. This design process allows the plant employee the opportunity to affect his or her portion of the business in such a way that innovation will make coming to work a more enriching experience than "just a job." In addition, some of the details on how documentation is maintained, the length of time between pay levels, and especially what is contained in each skill level, are vitally important to the employee. The proper structuring of these details gives the employee a chance to have some self determination in a skill area.

It sometimes happens that a component part of the work structure is developed that is not the plant manager's first choice, but is supported by the plant design team. It may also follow that the employees will ultimately work better under the team-supported plan. Keep an open mind. Ask yourself, is this plan addressing the desired result? There are many roads to the same goal. Most of the time, the important thing is not necessarily which path you go down, but whether you arrive or not.

Mid-Level or Department Management

The department manager plays a critical role in developing both employees and supervisors. Let's take a look at what the department managers should be doing as part of their normal duties:

° *Setting goals*
° *Keeping the teams informed*
° *Developing ways to enhance productivity*
° *Accepting criticism from plant management*

- *Making expectations clear*
- *Holding individuals and teams accountable for results*
- *Finding ways to enhance individual self-esteem*
- *Being a facilitator*
- *Determining and providing the needed resources*
- *Supporting the supervisors/crew leaders*
- *Upholding the integrity of the work system*
- *Thoroughly understanding the intent of the work system*
- *Developing skills in other managers*
- *Producing business results*

Providing leadership in these areas requires a lot of responsibility, but in order to be successful all of these factors must be present. The department manager must be perceived as a person who will listen, carefully consider the input, and respond with a clear answer. If you have a situation where a department manager does not support their supervisors and does not have a clear understanding of the manager's own role, that individual can deal a terrible blow to the success of your organization, whether it be traditional or high performance.

Support must come from the top down, and you should understand each individual's role in order to avoid a weak link. Certainly people are different and have different leadership styles, but the management duties listed above should be evaluated by the plant management and stated as performance criteria so that the department level manager knows what is expected for success.

Crew Leader / Supervisor

The supervisor or crew leader is commonly known as the person in the middle. This employee enforces company policy, helps employees with technical aspects of their jobs, serves as a counselor, motivator, and peacemaker, and generally keeps the crew in balance and focused on the business. Obviously the crew leader is an essential element in your business. This individual, by the very nature of the job assignment, has the greatest influence over how success is perceived by the employees in the organization's work structure.

My observation has been that these individuals are the least prepared to handle the change in work structure proposed in this book. A high performance work system needs high performance supervisors. For most employees, the most immediate impression of success comes from their supervisor or crew leader. In the same manner that your technicians must determine what success means within the system structure, the supervisors must also have a clear vision of that goal — not just for themselves, but also for the teams.

As a former supervisor, I can tell you from personal experience that most supervisors are utterly unprepared to handle the challenge that this type of system places squarely on their shoulders. Not every person is right for this role. Management should first look at the criteria that will make a successful supervisor in a high performance work system. Let's review the qualities and skills that these individuals should have:

- *Leadership ability*
- *Facilitation skills*
- *Team development skills*
- *Problem-solving skills*
- *Listening skills*
- *Technical skills*
- *Feedback training*
- *Confrontation training*

Perhaps you are thinking that the supervisors in your company already have these skills, but have they ever been asked to use them on a daily basis? Have they ever received formal training? If not, this type of training is readily available, and should be provided. Refer to the Appendix for more information about training resources.

Do not assume that your supervisors have these skills. Many of the supervisors I have known are fine people, yet because of their career history — being promoted from the ranks or hired directly out of college — they have never really had to deal with people in the way they will be asked to do in a high performance work structure. While it's bad enough to use unprepared supervisors in a traditional system, it can be a disaster in a high performance work structure.

There is one other essential quality that cannot be taught, and that is the willingness to change. The teams will invariably take on the personality of the supervisor, especially in the first years of the transition process. If the supervisor is not willing to change, he or she will have a negative affect on too many people, and should not be left in that critical position. Either move these individuals, or lose them, but do not look the other way.

"Move them or lose them" sounds harsh and I suppose it is, but let's look at a way other than training to help the supervisor make the transition to a new role. We'll start by considering the role of a supervisor in a more traditional work structure. We must understand their former responsibilities to understand what their new role should be.

Here is what a traditional supervisor does:

° *Plans coverage for work areas*
° *Disciplines employees for policy violations*
° *Provides technical help with the process*
° *Serves as a counselor for employees*
° *Facilitates at meetings*
° *Resolves conflicts*
° *Interacts with operations and maintenance*
° *Gathers outside resources for team*

- *Schedules training*
- *Supports management decisions*
- *Writes reports*

In a traditional system, the supervisor usually has a comprehensive job description. Initially this job description will not change much when going into a high performance work structure. As the supervisor and the team develop their skills under the high performance work structure, the supervisor's role may change greatly from the traditional. It even happens that the supervisor's role is no longer a necessary part of the team.

Supervisors in a high performance system must have an excellent understanding of the work structure and the reasoning behind it to be able to promote the concept. They must encourage active participation on the part of the employees, not by demanding, but by exercising good leadership techniques. It requires a paradigm shift in thinking to be able to manage people in a team environment. It's no wonder some people resist. After all, you are changing their perception of what success will be. And, it's easy to understand why a supervisor would not want to do more work — they have enough responsibility already! Supervisors who have experienced the type of system I am advocating will tell you their jobs are harder. On the other hand, their role is a lot more rewarding.

There is also one more very important goal in a high

performance work structure: *supervisors need to work themselves out of a job, by having the teams take over more and more responsibility.* At a minimum they must change the scope of their contribution to the organization. Why would anyone want to do that? They would not if they did not know how it was going to impact them in a positive way.

Each supervisor must have a goal, and management must define what success is for the supervisor. Some supervisors might someday be promoted to the next level of management — and that is a worthwhile goal — but it is important to align the supervisor's goal with the business of the company. So let me suggest a way to develop a success plan for each supervisor. Developing a plan for the supervisor should be done with his or her respective manager. First, with the supervisor present, develop a list of the supervisor's current job responsibilities, as shown in the example below. Then, with the supervisor, ask and answer the following question for each duty:

Which of these duties can your team accomplish if given proper training?

yes · *plan coverage for work areas*
no · *carry out discipline for policy violations*
  (but can make recommendations for discipline)
yes · *provide technical help with the process*

yes • serve as counselor
yes • facilitate meetings
yes • resolve conflicts
yes • interact with operations and maintenance
yes • gather outside resources for team
yes • schedule training
yes • support management decisions
yes • write reports

You will see that with training, it is possible for the team to get along without a supervisor in the traditional role. So what is there for the supervisor to do? At this point you actually begin to develop a plan by asking the supervisor: *How can you use your talents to contribute to the business? What would you like to do?* Here are some possible answers:

° *work on process improvement projects*
° *develop training for technicians*
° *do studies of statistical process control*
° *set up preventive maintenance systems*
° *carry out engineering studies*
° *be promoted to higher management*

There could be any number of things that the individual supervisor can and would like to do to supplement what is required for effective team performance. Obviously the answers depend on the person's background and interests. The point is to incorporate those personal desires that align with the company's needs into the supervisor's new responsibilities.

To develop a plan for success, give your supervisors a positive reason to work themselves out of a job. When evaluations are made for the supervisor, evaluate the team as well. Now the supervisor's success is directly tied to the team becoming self-sufficient. Define a time line and develop a strategy to address each item for which a team can assume responsibility. Study a team development model, then decide where each team should be and what new areas the team will take over.

But this is really jumping ahead to the implementation stage for teams. The point is to give your supervisors a goal from the very beginning. Give them a vested interest in making the system work.

The Most Important Person

The line employee, or technician, is the most important element in the mix. Their numbers are greater, and they are the ones that typically produce the end product, rather than a by-product or a service.

Why use the term *technician*? Why not *hourly employee* or *worker*? These and other terms are all descriptive, of course, and are variously used throughout industry. I prefer the word technician because this is the person who is being asked to do more in a high performance work structure. Particularly in Part 3, where I describe the process used to construct and implement this type of structure, I will use the term *technician* to refer to this level of employee.

Whether you are a technician, a manager, or a corporate head reading this book, make no mistake: It is simply about designing a structure that allows technicians and managers to contribute more toward making the organization a success. This concept challenges management to do more with people, and to use personal development to enhance the employees' self worth and the company's bottom line.

Chapter 5

Building Your Design Team

Designing a high performance work structure requires teamwork. Although you may use the services of consultants, the design process is not carried out by some group of specialists in some think tank. The design for your company or your plant within the company will be created by the people who will be working under the structure when it is implemented. We will call this design group the *plant design team*.

So, what is a plant design team? It is a group of people who work together to develop a work system that puts structure to the value statements of the organization. Yes, you will need to train the design team for this task, and training should be one of the first priorities. These people must develop the skills to perform as a team, which include:

- *Trust*
- *Decision making*
- *Problem solving*
- *Feedback*
- *Conflict resolution*
- *Listening*
- *Team building*

The plant design team will have a lot of information to process for your organization. Recommendations and decisions are part of the team's obligation. The facilitator you appoint should be qualified to develop all of the above training. It is less important for the facilitator to have a lot of experience with design and implementation, though some knowledge of the process is a benefit. One excellent starting point is team building exercises to help loosen up the group and familiarize the team members with one another. I guarantee, it will be tense enough at times as the team works through its assignment.

One quick comment on decision-making: Make sure that the group understands what is expected of them. There are three possibilities: Input, Recommendation, or Decision. Each of these carries a different level of decision-making authority. Misunderstandings can be painful if the team, for example, believes they are charged with making decisions when management only expects them to give input. Clarifying the assignment from the beginning will prevent misunderstandings at a later point.

From the start, the team should know how pay issues will be addressed. This could be by negotiation through the proper channels, or simply as a management decision that will be made after the process of design is completed. The design team is not a negotiation team, and there will be enough distractions for them without the money issue.

Do not have this group meet on site — get them away from the plant! Their whole focus needs to be on the task, not on daily work. Demand 100% attendance from team members, especially the managers who will be the most likely to try to slip out and take care of other issues. If this happens, it sends a clearly negative message to the technicians about how important the work system is to your organization. *A half-hearted effort will deliver a half-hearted product.*

Design Team Make-up

The optimum way to develop a design team is to involve the people who will be most affected by the new work structure. All levels of your current work environment should be considered. If the existing plant is a union plant, then that needs to be part of the criteria for participation on the plant design team. Thus the team should include not only union members, but also members of the union's executive committee.

If you have a non-union facility, then you should strive to include the informal leaders in the different work areas. You know who they are — ask them to participate! Another strategy is to invite nominations from the technicians. If a crew or team selects their own representatives, you are guaranteed to get some of these leaders.

It may also be advantageous to ask for volunteers on the design team, but do not rely completely on this approach. If you try to staff your team strictly through volunteers, you may get some people who do not have much credibility with their peers. Do not underestimate the type of person you need on the team. The technicians selected for the design teams must be willing to speak-up about any issue the design team brings to the table.

Let's look at one possible make-up of a plant design team:

° **Management**
 · one department-level manager
 · one middle manager
 · three supervisors(one maintenance\operational)
° **Technicians**
 · two per shift team (operations)

• two from maintenance crews

Thus, an ideal size for the plant design would include about five managers and ten technicians. This scenario assumes your operations crews have an average of about fifteen persons per shift team. Naturally you can adjust this based on the size of your facility, but try to stay within the optimum range of eight to fifteen persons on the team. The process normally needs to be broken into sub-groups to proceed in a timely manner, and a team of less than eight does not lend itself to splitting responsibilities. The most important consideration here is that you have the correct mix of individuals from the different disciplines, as they all have something to contribute.

You will need one other person involved with this group: a facilitator. The ideal facilitator is one that can impartially guide the group and keep them focused on the task at hand throughout the process. This person should not make decisions or even recommendations, but just simply guide the process. In addition to facilitation skills, the facilitator should be able to handle the training in the following areas:

° *Team development model*
° *Listening skills*
° *Conflict resolution*
° *Feedback*

° *Problem solving*
° *Decision making principles*

A facilitator should have experience in teaching these skills, not one who plans to learn on the job. In the end you will need trainers in your ranks as well and this is a good opportunity to bring the design team up to speed on training techniques.

You may have realized that I did not recommend the plant manager be on the team. The plant manager should give direction and narrow the scope given by the corporate leadership, but should not be directly involved in the design. The plant manager usually cannot commit the amount of continuous time that will be required, and that would lead the participants into thinking the overall commitment was not there. However, the plant manager should schedule regular meetings with the entire group to discuss issues as they arise. The design team may want to challenge some of the parameters set by the plant manager, or have the plant manager clarify the position on some issue. Frequent meetings to discuss these issues will keep the lines of communication open.

Where to start?

The plant design team has a lot of areas to consider in

carrying out their assignment. Before we get any further into the design, we must take a closer look at the role of the plant design team. This team needs to be the umbrella, under which all departments of your plant will operate under. At the same time, the plant design team must be constantly aware of the various departments or sections of the plant. Those departments will need the opportunity to maneuver within the design.

The plant design team function will be related to the direction for the plant as a whole, and should not allow too much detail to the individual business departments as to restrict their design process. If your organization is made up of just one section or business department, then the plant team can design the overall structure and provide the details as well. I will explain the detail for the departments and the department design teams as we proceed through the process.

Our goal, then, is to create an umbrella for the plant direction. Remember the umbrella diagram in Chapter 3. The different spines of the umbrella will be the major categories that the design team will address. The handle of the umbrella is the plant management's direction as given to the design team. The fabric of the umbrella is the detail that the plant adds on by a department-by-department basis. What area should we start on first? Who should be responsible for what? Now the training the facilitator as given the group will be tested. Now you will also see how the make-up of the design team comes into play. In order to come up with the best possible product, you need the perspective of the technicians, supervisors, middle and upper management.

Department-Level Teams

A good mix of skills is essential when you set up you plant design team, because here comes another payoff. This will become more apparent as we work to put the fabric on the umbrella structure. For a good mix on the department level team, I included a supervisor, some technicians, and a department manager if possible. The same types of persons you sent to the plant design team need to be a part of the department design team.

The umbrella framework has for the most part been formulated. Now the real pressure starts, especially for the technicians. After all, we are designing how a technician receives promotions. In addition, we are presenting change and it seems that for the most part that is stressful, simply because of fear of the unknown.

The department design team will primarily be determined by the shift teams. Depending on the size of the shift teams, it would be good at least initially to have two technicians per shift assigned to this team. For purposes of this book, I have assumed that the shift teams have between ten and twenty persons per team. You can adjust the number of representatives down to one technician per shift team, but this would be the minimum. Two is a better selection as it would help to take communication more reliable. Don't forget the day team if you have one in the department. The people that were assigned to the plant design team should be sprinkled in with others from your department, as this will help you avoid duplicating efforts later in the design of your work structure.

With these considerations in mind, the department design team should look something like this:

° **Shift Teams:**
- A — 2 technicians
- B — 2 technicians
- C — 2 technicians
- D — 2 technicians
- Day team — 2 technicians

° 1 or 2 **shift supervisors**(one from the site team)

° **Department Manager** should be on this team whether this person was on the plant design team or not.

How should the technicians be selected? They should be chosen by their peers from the teams they are representing. When selecting technicians, be sure you get a cross section of the type of skills your group will be dealing with, ie., both operational and maintenance. It's important that your design teams include the informal leaders from each shift team or work crew. These people will lend credibility to the process.

The shift supervisors will give the group some real world balance. The supervisor knows the job assignments and thus can add some necessary balance when the group gets into the issues it will be required to wrestle with.

The department-level manager is there to ensure that the goals of the department are always considered in work system decisions. Equally important, the department manager is there to show support for the work system, period. It will be obvious, if the department manager does not attend the meetings and does not participate in making recommendations, that he or she is not committed to the effort. Do not let this happen! As with the plant design team, attendance should be a basic expectation.

One other person should be at the initial meetings, and that person is the facilitator. The facilitator's role is to assure that the dynamics of the group are working in the right direction, to lay out the subject areas and goals of the group, and to remind the group that their job is to add the *"fabric"* to the plant umbrella, that is, the details that are specific to the individual departments.

The facilitator should also train the group. I can almost hear you saying: What? Training again? The training should include, first, the role of the department design team and the elements of the plant design. The facilitator's job will be to have everyone on the same page, and to make sure there is no debate on the elements already decided at the plant level. I guarantee that the people not involved with the previous decisions will want to know what was behind them.

The department design team should be given the same training the plant team received in team building, decision making, problem solving, feedback, conflict resolution, and listening skills. This additional training will help build a bond between the members of the department design team. Since the persons who were on the plant design team have already been trained in these skills, you may want to consider letting some of the team members do this training without the aid of the facilitator. This will give the facilitator more time to assist the other departments.

Communication by Design

As your company proceeds through the design process, you must constantly ask yourself and the design teams, *what does this design say to the people in the system?* What is the perception that we think this will convey? Will it be perceived as fair? Does it have integrity built into the system, or is it just giving lip service?

When any organization undertakes a potential change, the rumors will run wild. Your design group should spend some time developing a plan to share information with the shift teams that will be affected by the work system change — not just the technicians, but the management team as well. Communication will occur naturally as your design team receives information from the shift teams about the specific skills in their work process, but this is not enough.

Information sharing meetings should be held at convenient times for all employees to attend. Make sure these meetings are held in a central location at your site. Make the meeting like a rap session, but structure it with prepared information at the beginning. Hold a question and answer session towards the end and have these meetings at least once a week.

At each meeting, the communication should to be structured in a way that allows an open forum of information, questions and answers. The design team should agree on the information package content, and a mix of people from the design team should be present to deliver the message.

You cannot completely stop rumors, but you can halt the process by giving out accurate and consistent information at each meeting.

Chapter 6

Design Considerations for a New Plant

In a large manufacturing facility in the eastern U.S., the top managers made a decision to develop a progressive work structure for a new plant. They envisioned a work structure that would positively affect business results and produce an energetic work force. All the managers involved in this progressive work structure were convinced that it was the right thing to do. The support was so enthusiastic that when they hired the all-new work force, it was insinuated that the only criterion for success in this system was the employee's own initiative. The management staff did not go into great detail about what the real promotional criteria were.

Naturally, the newly hired employees were enthusiastic about working for a company that was so progressive.

Naturally, all the employees knew that they would move to the top quickly. After all, everyone understands that testing and demonstrating skills is a natural way to get promoted. Right?

Well, the majority of employees in the new work force thought, *I will just work hard and that's all there is to it.* As with most jobs, the reality eventually revealed that, in fact, it is a job, and getting promoted required a concentrated effort on the part of the employee. For this company, the "concentrated effort" included documentation of tests, task demonstrations, and even a review by the employee's peers.

There was a loud hue and cry, with employees complaining that management did not tell them about this: *It's not utopia, it is just another job and not an easy one at that!"* The employees viewed the situation, not as progression at their own pace, but progression at the company's pace. And that was not what they were told when they were hired!

Take heed of this example. While most of the employees at that manufacturing facility now understand that the system for promotion is fair, they will tell you to this day that they were lied to by management. While management did not intentionally mislead the employees, this example shows what kind of effect an early misunderstanding may have on an organization.

Do not paint a *rosy* picture to your employees — give it to them straight. If it's fair they will see it, and if it does happen to turn out better than they expect, that will be perceived as a bonus. Give your employees credit for being able to make a decision about your work structure simply based on the facts. *A rosy picture will soon wilt, while a realistic picture will stand the test of time.*

While the design process for a new plant will be similar to the overall procedure outlined in this book, there are some differences.

Plant Management

The plant or site management at a new location has an involved role in designing the work system structure. Unlike the existing plants, in a new site the plant manager should be part of the plant design team. In addition to determining the specific direction for the plant and interpreting the corporate direction, the plant manager has the opportunity to incorporate considerable detail into the general recommendations.

Because it is a new plant, the plant manager has the opportunity to hire all new staff, from department level managers on down to the technicians. This gives management a tremendous opportunity to hire the type of individual who shares the same general philosophy about a work structure that is based on contribution to the organization. It will be tempting to describe the work structure to the new employees in a rosy light, but, as shown by the prior example that opened this chapter, this has its pitfalls.

In fact, you should consider describing your work structure in a way that makes it sound rather difficult to achieve success. That way, when employees succeed beyond their expectations, their perception will be positive. Besides, you want people who are willing to tackle a challenge.

Because the plant is in a start-up situation, your employees' concentration should be on getting the site *"up and running,"* that is, operational and productive, rather than on implementing the new work structure. I am not saying do not do any of the design work, but I suggest that you do not implement it for a period of time. Complete the initial design structure so you can explain it to the employees, when you hire them, about how the promotion pattern will work. Then, set a time frame before you implement the high performance work structure. In addition to the time frame, set a quality/production-related goal. Typically a good rule of thumb would be minimum of one year before the high performance work structure can start under any conditions, assuming that the quality and production goals have been accomplished.

Department Managers

As in the case of the plant manager at a new plant, the department level managers also have an opportunity to make a dramatic effect on the work structure. We all realize that some of the management staff will be selected not to manage people, but to work on projects or perform strictly technical jobs. A word of warning: If you do not apply some people-management criteria to all managers, it will come back to haunt you.

Some of the technical managers will want to move into positions that deal more directly with people. These people should be evaluated on their ability to interact with people as well as on their technical expertise. Of course you can always complete or perform the evaluations as the job opportunities open up, but why not do it on the front end? Do not think that your managers will not affect the perception of the work structure. You need proponents, not opponents.

Supervisors/Team Leaders

Of all the employees that the department manager will hire, the ones who will have the greatest impact on the success of the work structure are the supervisors. The new work force that you hire will reflect the supervisor's personality. Make sure you hire the type of supervisor who reflects the results you want for your department.

At a new plant, you have the opportunity to select supervisors who have a better chance of fitting this new management style, with this type of work structure. The attributes you look for in a supervisor are not inconsistent, no matter what type of system you use. However, if you hire solely on technical merit, without placing strong consideration on leadership qualities, you will regret it.

If you are honest with yourself, you'll acknowledge that the technicians, in time, will be able to assume the role of providing technical expertise in the operation of the equipment. This is even more the case with the work structure proposed here, where the technicians will have multiple skills.

The Technicians

In addition to hiring the management staff in developing a new organization, management must consider the technician work force and the options associated with hiring. I have heard over and over how important the technicians are to any organization, and yet in many instances you still see little or no evaluation of their compatibility with the company's work structure. If in fact they are such a vital part of an organization's success, then the characteristics of a good technician had better be understood.

There are two major options that management has when hiring a new work force:

1. You can hire an all-green work force, i.e., a work force that you intentionally hire that has no experience in your industry.

2. *You can hire some technicians who have experience in your industry.*

Let's take a look at the pro's and con's of the two options:

Option 1: All-green technician work force
- ° Advantages
    - · No paradigms about your particular industry
    - · Learn the technical process your way
    - · Equal opportunity for all employees
    - · No perceived job classifications by technicians

- ° Disadvantages
    - · Initial training a lot more intense
    - · Potentially a longer start-up curve
    - · More pressure on technical ability of supervisor
    - · Supervisor paradigms become team paradigms

Option 2: Hiring skilled help for some positions

- ° Advantages
    - · More technical help on start-up

- Less technical reliance on supervisor
- Should shorten start-up curve

° Disadvantages
- Brings more industry paradigms
- Limits opportunity in key jobs for new technicians
- Will create lines of division between experienced and new employees.

As you can see, both options have their merits. Depending on the technology for your industry, you must weigh the pro's and con's. If you are willing to give up some of the short-term gains, I would suggest you strongly consider hiring an all-green work force.

Design Team Make-up

At this juncture you do not have technicians, so your management staff should be the design team. In this situation I would suggest that the plant manager assume a more active role in the plant design team's activities — not as the leader of the group but as a contributor to the design.

Because of this recommendation, the need for a facilitator is vital. The training of the group is still necessary, as it will loosen the group up and perhaps allow a more relaxed exchange of ideas.

Part 3

High Performance

How It Gets Done

Chapter 7

Getting Started

Starting from the beginning, your design teams should be given a common vocabulary to use in discussing the new system. I gave an overview of the components of the high performance work structure earlier, in Part I. Now let's look in more detail at the basic "building blocks" of the system. These are:

° *Levels*
° *Skill sets*
° *Task areas or Modules*

With reference to levels, I am talking about the combination and/or amount of skill required to gain a higher rate of pay. When I refer to a particular skill set, that is the specific technical information required for a pay increase. The individual elements of a skill set will be called task areas or modules. Exhibit D will give a graphic display of the relationship.

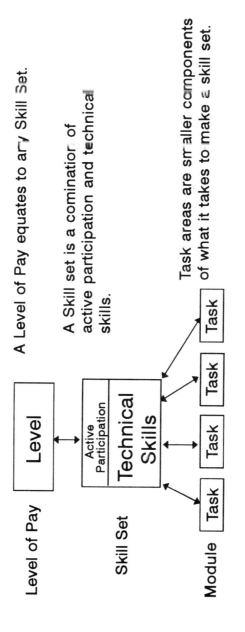

A level can be any one of a group of skill sets. A skill set comprises all the technical requirements of the particular combination of modules in that skill set. Task areas are the individual elements that make up a skill set. You can call these building blocks or anything you want, as long as the relationships are understood.

The charge for the team is to evaluate the existing way the organization does business, and to assign as much of the existing work structure as possible to these "building blocks." Each task area your company needs to perform in order to carry out its business should be evaluated. The tasks that the company performed under the old work structure will generally not change, but, under the new system, how they are accomplished and by whom may change dramatically. The design team that works on this issue will need to have some resource person or contact available with the different task areas.

A critical need in this process is to establish a valid determination of the technical skills that should be assigned to each level, including the degree of skill and the time that it should take for the "average" technician to progress from level to level. While it is true that time will no longer be the predominating factor controlling employee movement or progression, it will still be a factor. To overlook the role of time in the new system would be foolish indeed. You therefore should look at time as a way to balance the skill sets, and you will see more about this in the next chapter under calibration of the skill sets. But time in this case is used with a very specific meaning, and no longer refers to "time on the job," allowing movement only when someone dies, retires or quits.

Gathering Information

The next step is for the plant design team is to begin gathering information that will help them in the process. One of the best ways to do this is to send the design team out to visit other companies that have made the transition. Learning from others' successes and mistakes is a lot more efficient than repeating the same mistakes over and over again.

Some homework is in order before the plant visits begin. First, develop a list of locations with progressive work structures. Utilizing a Human Resource Management association would be a good starting point. Some associations are listed in the appendix. Remember there are organizations out there that claim to be non-traditional, but are so in name only. After developing a list, look at the values your organization deems important. It will be beneficial to talk to some of the locations prior to making a visit.

At this stage, it may be hard to know what questions to ask about work systems. In Exhibit E at the end of this chapter, I have compiled a list of questions that address all the components of design. By using these questions when visiting the other organizations, it will help you become aware of *"the good, the bad, and the ugly"* before you design the wrong factors into your system. Asking the right questions at least improves your chance of receiving the right answers.

Now that the plant design team is armed with these questions and any others that may be pertinent to your company, it's time to gather information. Divide your group into equal teams, and send each team to a different plant. This method will allow your design team to quickly gain a perspective. Each plant-visit group should include both managers and technicians. Approximately one manager and three technicians is a good mix for gaining this perspective. Each group decides on the specific questions for their survey of the sites. The only dumb question is the one that you did not ask, and that question could have saved you some grief in the future.

Before your visit, ask the host company to give you about a day — approximately six to eight hours' worth of time — with a tour included, if possible. The tour will allow your group to ask some questions on the floor of the operation, if possible.

It would be great if you could arrange two plant visits per group. This may not be possible, however, because as you survey your industry, you may find that not many have ventured in the direction you are heading. Fear not and press on, for the reward can be great! Look at examples from outside your specific industry, as well. After all, your system needs to be *unique* to you and because it is yours, this ownership in the end will be a strength.

Remember, the more information the team members have in the beginning, the better the job they can do. Each team should bring back their information and put it into categories for the different groups that will be made up to design your system. Make sure the questions and answers are available to all team members, because the information will be applicable to several design areas.

If you are designing a work structure for a new plant, you will have to rely on your management staff to gather this information. If possible, try to include as many supervisors as possible in this process. Remember, theirs is the management level that will have the greatest interaction with the technicians. All the other questions presented in this section are still valid, and will provide a base for good decisions in your future design efforts.

Exhibit E. Questions to ask other organizations about their transition to a high performance work structure.

1. *How many levels of skill can a person attain?*
2. *What are the component parts of a skill in your system?*

3. How did you address flexibility in designing your system?
4. How long is the average time between pay levels?
5. How do you evaluate skills?
6. How does your training process work?
7. Who evaluates skills?
8. How did you calibrate skills?
9. What kind of training did your design team receive?
10. How did you communicate with the plant's employees about the design of the work system?
11. What factor did time have in your system?
12. Do you expect people to maintain and utilize their skills?
13. Why did you change to this type of work structure?
14. How has the work system helped with productivity?
15. How has the work system rewarded the people who actually contribute more?
16. How did you determine how many of each skill you needed?
17. What role do the technicians have in promotion?
18. How do you handle rotation of skills?
19. What is the difference between maintenance and operations, if any?
20. Does your system have caps?
21. How did you give credit for previous skills?
22. How do you determine what job function each person will be assigned?

23. How do you handle openings for new employees?
24. What do you do when someone calls in sick?
25. How do determine who trains next?
26. Who decides what skills each individual will get?
27. What do you expect besides technical skills?
28. How does your plant define fairness?
30. What percentage of time is dedicated to training?
31. How did you make the transition from the old system to the new work structure?
32. What are the components of your skill sets?
33. How are differences settled?
34. How did or do you combat job ownership?
35. How are decisions made within operating teams?
36. How does someone say "I have progressed as far through the system as I would like?"
37. How do you handle requests for time off, vacations, etc?
38. How many employees does your system cover?
39. How do you handle licensing issues?
40. What do you expect in the area of leadership?
41. How do you define active participation?
42. What type of incentives do you have to motivate people?
43. Do you have team meetings?
44. What do you do in your team meetings?
45. Who does evaluations of employee performance?
46. How are your certification/promotion boards set up?

47. How do you handle movement between departments?
48. How can people still use their skills if they change departments?
49. Can people lose skills?
50. Who chooses the particular skills a person attains?
51. Do you treat people equally in your system?
52. How has this system increased productivity?
53. How has it impacted safety?
54. Did the shift schedule have a role in the design?
55. How do you deal with non contributors?
56. What hiring techniques do you use?
57. Are the teams involved in discipline?
58. What is the role of the shift supervisor?
59. Who had the most problems with the change and why?
60. Did some people quit?
61. Who benefitted most?
62. What happens when a person gets to the top?
63. Do you promote internally?
64. What would you change if you could?
65. How often do you evaluate your system to see if it is working as designed?
66. How do you handle change in the work system?
67. How does your promotion process ensure integrity?
68. What is the role of the supervisor?
69. What is the role of the department manager?
70. How does the plant manager support the work structure?

Chapter 8

Calibration and Skill Set Building

One of the subgroups of the design team will have the challenge of deciding how to calibrate the various task areas already present in the company or plant. The calibration group should be prepared to view each job task from a different perspective than they have in the past. As mentioned earlier, traditional job classifications only address two criteria: First, what is the smallest safe operation that a single employee can do and still be productive? Second, how are these tasks arranged from least desirable up to the physically easiest or more mentally demanding? This is the typical mind-set in traditional systems, and has been the norm for many years.

In contrast, the calibration group needs to develop a tool

that will accomplish several things. It must allow technicians to evaluate task areas against a standard, and allow management to pay the technicians based upon that standard. The standard must be applied fairly, based upon individual accomplishments and business needs. The calibration step will set the tone of the new system. Therefore, it is critical because it really dictates what technical skills the company values as an organization. Make no mistake, this exercise will generate a lot of emotion in the organization! A task that someone has been doing for years always seems to grow in importance to the individual who is doing it, and that individual can become very emotional when his or her work area is examined objectively. The first time the team comes into contact with this situation, the employees' emotional responses may give more weight to the task than there really is. That is why the calibration tool must be designed fairly and applied consistently across the board.

The job of the calibration group, is to develop a method to evaluate technical skills that are clear, understandable, and will deliver results. Furthermore, the employees as a whole must perceive it as being a fair system. The calibration tool must be consistent, and it must be measurable if it is to have any consistency. All right, just what is important to measure when calibrating the skills required to perform a specific task? Here are some questions the calibration group might ask:

Please Die - I Want A Promotion

1. *How long does it take to learn the technical aspects of the task and perform it acceptably?*
2. *How does the task impact the business?*
3. *What level of decision-making is required for the task?*
4. *What type of environment does the person work in when performing the task?*
5. *What are the physical requirements of the task?*

Are these factors all the elements of a good calibration? They could be; that is one of the decisions the team will have to make depending on their particular situation. Obviously I think they are important considerations; I could not imagine a calibration process that did not contain at least some of the above elements. However, these five factors are not equal when you consider relative importance. The attachment of weight to each element will allow the calibration group to customize the tool to their organization. One company may be very heavy in the technical side, but light in physical activity. Another company may not even need to consider the physical part. The environment may not be a consideration if the plant interior is more like an office. There may not be any heavy decision-making if procedures have to be strictly followed because of safety or other considerations. You have to evaluate your specific needs. Some of these considerations may fit your organization, and you may have to add others.

The weighing of these categories sends a message about

the relative importance (or value) of skills. Each team's weighing system will differ, depending on the needs of the organization. For purposes of illustration, let's set up a weighing system to be used by the calibration group from "Company B."

Point Value System

1. *Time needed to learn technology*   *1 week = 5 points*
2. *Impact on the business*   scale 1 - 20
3. *Decision making*   scale 1 - 15
4. *Environment*   scale 1 - 10
5. *Physical requirements*   scale 1 - 10

Note that the items are not weighted equally and are not all scaled in the same way, but all of them have a point value. I placed the most weight on the length of time it takes to train, as this is usually the least subjective of the measurements that a typical calibration group will use. Now let's take a scenario and apply this point value system to a particular task area.

Example 1:

Task area: Fork Truck Operator

1. *Time to train*   *3 weeks = 15 points*
2. Decision making   7 points
3. Impact on business   6 points
4. Environment   8 points
5. Physical demands   9 points
   Total   45 points

Notice that training time (that is, the technical basis of the task) is given the greatest weight. It takes three weeks to bring this person up to speed, giving a point value of 15. Decision-making, on a scale of 1 to 20, is given the score of 7, which indicates that most of the decisions are already laid out for this task. An example of decision-making here occurs when the operator has a variety of load patterns and must decide on the right load pattern to use according to the application. However, there may only be four different load patterns to deal with.

Factor 4, impact on the business, is given a lower score because the product is already made. While it is important that the product gets to the customer in good condition, there are a limited number of choices that would cause issues with the product. Physical requirements are rated somewhat higher because the operator has to drive all day and prepare truck and rail cars for shipment. It is a very physical task area.

Example 2:

Task area: Tester

1. Time to train   8 weeks = 40 points
2. Decision making   15 points
3. Impact on business   5 points
4. Environment   3 points
5. Physical demands   2 points
   Total   65 points

In this example, the work is more technical in nature, and the decision-making component is very important. The impact on the business is in the mid range. Both the environment and the physical requirements are minimal for "Tester" task area.

Example 3:

Task area: Control Room Operator

1. Time to train 15 weeks = 75 points
2. Decision making   15 points
3. Impact on business   9 points
4. Environment   3 points
5. Physical demands   2 points
    Total   104 points

This example is even more technical in nature. The employee is controlling a process, perhaps by using a distributed control system. It takes 15 weeks to complete the training and reach an acceptable level of operating skill. Decision making is significant, as this task requires constant monitoring. Many decisions must be made each hour to keep the process running within specifications. Impact on the business is high, as the decisions that the operator makes can make or break a productive run of product. Environment is scored low, as the operator works in an air-conditioned control room. Physical demands are minimal, as the task does not have very many demands other than changing out computer paper or walking to do an equipment check.

Looking at these three examples, it is evident that the

allocation of point values will be extremely important to the organization. After all, the calibration tells your people what their contribution means to the company. By applying this process, the design group will ultimately complete a calibration on every task area in the plant. This process sets up the relationships that the team will use to determine what goes into each skill set.

Before proceeding, the plant design team should "calibrate" the calibration tool. By following the examples presented, and selecting several task areas from the different departments in your plant. Chose tasks that will allow a variety of outcomes, and test the calibration tool. Use the tool to apply the point value system with the categories the team has established. When the plant team is finished, they will notice a relationship between the different task areas. Does the relationship seem right? If it does, then go with it.

When the team actually begins the calibration for the plant, I recommend that the entire plant design team be trained in the calibration process, and the whole team participate in the calibration of the skills. The group will need the feedback from the entire team to make a good decision for each task area. Each area should be represented on the design team. We will look again at the task calibration issue when we begin working with the individual team and department areas. Now, for more concepts of design.

Relatively Equal

While working through the design process, the company and the design team must continually ask themselves, what does this system we are developing say to the people in it? Will it be perceived as fair? Is the concept of "relatively equal" clearly understood by all participants? By all the participants, I mean everyone at the site from the plant manager on down.

This concept is extremely important in several areas that I will detail for you. Now, I'm doing it again; I'm getting back to saying things should be equal! However, in this case, I want to distinguish between the traditional systems, which attempt to treat people as if they were "equal" or "the same," and the high performance work structure, which makes the *skill sets* equal. Making skill sets equal will help us distinguish those characteristics that differentiate between people.

Why is it important to have equal skill sets? Simply put, it helps get the message across about what is valued in the organization. It aligns the skills properly according to what the business wishes to have accomplished. Here is the message you will send by having relatively equal skill sets:

1. *All grouped skills have value.*
2. *There is no right or wrong progression pattern.*
3. *Skill sets will be aligned to business needs.*

Please Die - I Want A Promotion

4. *All components of skills are a shared responsibility.*
5. *Equal levels blur traditional lines of progression.*
6. *Accounting will be simplified by eliminating dozens of pay increments.*
7. *The "one job, one person" syndrome will be eliminated.*

Remember you are sending a message with each part of your system design.

So how do you make all skill sets relatively equal? In the previous step, the design team developed a way to calibrate the different task areas and assign them a point value. The next step is to determine how many points should be in a level.

Keep in mind there are many acceptable ways to accomplish this step. This is one of the strengths of the high performance work structure; it not only guides the work being done, but encourages innovation in the way it is accomplished. There are two extremes you must avoid:

1. Skill sets available at any time to anyone.
2. Skill sets unavailable and unattainable.

Here, I am talking about an employee in a high performance work structure obtaining a new skill set, not making the transition from the traditional system.

One of the pitfalls in system design is not to consider the

relationship of skill sets. While structuring the number of levels that will be in the new system, the design team should keep in mind this concept does not mean that every employee will have every skill set in a particular department. The fact is, a person at a relatively high level before the transition could have half or two-thirds of the new skill sets. It's a good idea to put plenty of substance into each skill set, and make several skill sets available to the department's employees.

We have already discussed some examples showing how to set up a valuation method for the technical aspects of the work. We will continue to use the technical side for now as we go through some examples of how to develop skill sets. Later we will blend in Active Participation as we tie the system together.

When the team develops its skill sets, I suggest that between four and nine levels be made available to the technicians. The number you develop will, of course, be defined by the point value system the team has developed. For our purposes, we will use six levels for "Company B." The number of levels you design into your system should be enough to stretch even the most able and willing employees capability. Keep in mind that just because you have a six-level system that does not mean you only have six skill sets throughout the business. It is common to have 10 to 15 different skill sets, per department, depending on the company's calibration criteria.

Recall the task area examples of Fork Truck Operator, Tester, and Control Room Operator. The Fork Truck Operator was valued by our calibration system at 45 points. The Tester was valued at 65 points. The Control Room Operator was valued at 104 points. Next, for example the design group decides that a level should consist of 60 to 65 points. This means that the Control Room Operator has enough points in that position to reach almost two levels of pay. That would be almost two skill sets for that particular business department.

The Fork Truck task area would have to be combined with another related task area to add enough point value to reach the 60-point minimum. The Tester skill area was calibrated to 65 points, which is sufficient value to reach one level.

Following this concept, the grouping of similar or related tasks will begin to make all the skill sets in the business department relatively equal. I use the term *"relatively"* because, no matter how hard you try, people will perceive some skill sets as harder or easier than others. This will happen for various reasons, such as someone enjoying the work more, or because it was harder for an individual to learn. Do the best you can to equalize the skill sets — it will pay off in the long run. We will further balance out the skill sets when we get into team responsibilities, as we must then make sure that the balance of skills is appropriate for each business department.

Active Participation

What defines Active Participation in your organization? Does it simply mean doing a specific job technically well? In a high performance work structure, active participation means a lot more than physically performing a job function. Active participation is a combination of leadership, interpersonal skills, and generally going beyond the technical task to enhance the organization's productivity.

The role of Active Participation needs to be designed into the pay levels so that everyone in the organization can, and is expected to, participate at some level. If company direction establishes that this is a fundamental principle for the organization, then the design group should determine if participation is to be linear or exponential. Should it be, the more you get paid the more participation is expected, or should it be the same amount of Active Participation at each level of pay, or some other combination? Each method has it merits.

Though a guideline is necessary in order to assess Active Participation, it is important for the goals that the company expects people to accomplish be a natural order of business. Active Participation, should add value to the organization. What will be the requirements of active participation? Here are some activities that could be included in a company's Active Participation requirements. The team should make a list of anything they can think of, other than the technical performance of the task.

Such as participating in:

- *Team meetings*
- *Training others*
- *Cost committee meetings*
- *Evaluating work system*
- *Serving on safety committee*
- *Filling in for supervisor*
- *Completing special projects*
- *Serving on emergency response teams*
- *Giving community service*
- *Hiring new employees*
- *Problem solving meetings*
- *Certification boards for promotion*

There is something for everyone. The trouble with most organizations is that only a few technicians participate in most of these activities. What a waste! Not only do the few people who participate get burned out, but the organization loses the ideas that others can provide. After all, with more people generating new ideas, the company can become more productive. The design team should look for as many different ways as possible for the company's technicians to show Active Participation.

You will notice that I listed community service. Sure, all companies want to be community-minded, but how many give their people credit for participation in a local fire department, a community fund raising effort, a local hospital, or whatever? The employees will appreciate it and the organization will receive a lot of mileage out of it with the community.

In many companies, the management settles for whatever participation they can get by the volunteer method, and this gradually slows to a trickle. Keep the participation flowing by putting it in the work structure. I am not trying to imply, Active Participation is more important or even equal to the technical requirements of the job. It does, however, have real value and is an excellent opportunity to gain something you do not have now. Look at Active Participation as the cream on top of a cup of hot chocolate. That little change adds so much to the product.

Skill Set Components Relationship

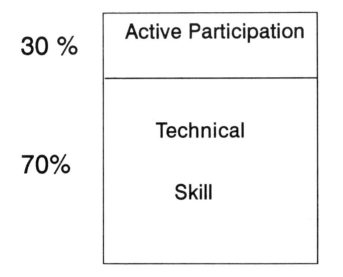

30 % Active Participation

70% Technical Skill

Exhibit F

To demonstrate how to calibrate Active Participation, let's continue with the skill set example from Company B. The team has decided to value Active Participation as 30 percent of the total skill set, and the technical part as 70 percent.

The subgroup of the design team that works on this very subjective topic has several ways to develop a finished product. The design team should assure the relative value is appropriate to the level of pay, that is, the number of skill sets a person has attained. In our example, the Company B team decides to break down the items listed previously in the following way:

° **Team meetings**
   1. Participation in the meeting
   2. Leading a team meeting
   3. Being responsible for a specific topic
° **Training**
   1. One-on-one
   2. One to group (structured format)
° **Cost committee**
   1. Team level
   2. Department level
   3. Plant Level
° **Work system committee**
   1. Team level
   2. Department level

3. Plant level
- **Safety committee**
  1. Team level
  2. Department level
  3. Plant level
- **Supervisor fill-in**
  1. Day
  2. Week
  3. Month
- **Special project**
  1. Team level
  2. Department level
  3. Plant Level
- **Emergency response team**
  1. Fire suppression member
  2. Hazard response member
  3. Rescue member
- **Community service**
  1. Local charity
  2. Teacher's aide
  3. Others
- **Problem solving**
  1. Team level
  2. Department level
  3. Plant level
- **Certification board member**
  1. Team level

2. Department level
3. Plant level
- **Hiring**
  1. Plant interview team

These examples show the potential for employees to actively participate in a variety of areas and at different levels of involvement. The way to ask for what the team has defined as Active Participation, is to assign a point value to each level of participation. Whatever value the team decides will work as long as it is applied consistently. For this example, we will use a 1 to 4 point scoring method and assign values to each activity. The actual point value is unimportant; it is how fairly the program is administered that will dictate its results or lack of results.

Now it's time to assign the active participation requirements to the pay levels. Company B uses 6 levels of pay, which will fit the needs of most organizations. In this first example, the point requirement for each level increases as the levels increase. The subjects listed under each level are examples of how different employees could fulfill the requirements for that level.

Level 1 / Requirement 5 points
   Team meetings   *2 points*
   Dept. Certification Board   *3 points*

Level 2 / Requirement 7 points
   Team meetings   *2 points*
   Dept. Certification Board   *3 points*
   Emergency Response (Fire) *2 points*

Level 3 / Requirement 9 points
   Team meetings   *2 points*
   Dept. Certification Board   *3 points*
   Emergency Response (fire) *2 points*
   Supervisor fill-in   *2 points*

Level 4 / Requirement 11 points
   Safety Trainer (site)   *4 points*
   Hiring (site)   *4 points*
   Cost Committee (dept.) *3 points*

Level 5 / Requirement 13 points
   Safety Trainer (site)   *4 points*
   Supervisor fill-in   *2 points*
   Department Project   *3 points*
   Team meetings   *2 points*
   Team project   *2 points*

Level 6 / Requirement 15 points
  Emergency Response (fire)   2 points
  Certification board member   4 points
  Community service   4 points
  Cost Committee (dept.)   3 points
  Supervisor fill-in   2 points

As this example shows, how a person actively participates can be very different at each level. Each individual has many options. Please keep in mind, however, that when I list items such as meetings, I do not mean just attending but *participating*. One way to evaluate this, is to have the meeting leader's input regarding an individual's participation. Normally I would say this is unnecessary, since most people who become involved are genuinely interested in the activity. Also, if the meeting facilitator has good skills, he or she will require everyone to participate.

A second way to incorporate active participation into the pay levels is to allocate an equal number of points to each level. For example, the team may require 9 points per level. This will ask for some amount of active participation from each individual, and the items can still vary depending on the person's interest. However, this method may emphasize the lower-point items and lead to a somewhat lowered expectation among the employees regarding active participation.

Level 1 / Requirement 9 points
   Safety Trainer (dept.)   *3 points*
   Dept. Certification Board   *3 points*
   Project participation   *3 points*

Level 2 / Requirement 9 points
   Safety Trainer (dept.)   *3 points*
   Meeting leader (dept.)   *3 points*
   Community involvement   *4 points*

Level 3 / Requirement 9 points
   Cost Committee (dept.)   *3 points*
   Emergency Response (fire)   *2 points*
   Team training   *2 points*
   Certification Board   *2 points*

Level 4 / Requirement 9 points
   Supervisor fill-in   *2 points*
   Safety Trainer (dept.)   *3 points*
   Design team (site)   *4 points*

Level 5 / Requirement 9 points
   Hiring   *4 points*
   Training (one-on-one)   *1 point*
   Community service   *4 points*

Level 6 / Requirement 9 points
  Community service   4 points
  Certification board (site) 4 points
  Training (one-on-one)   1 point

This example shows three or four types of Active Participation in each level. However, you could just as easily have five or six different items per level. Do not get hung up on making sure you hit the exact number of points, which in this case is 9. Just make sure the minimum acceptable number of points is understood.

A third way to handle Active Participation is through a combination of the above methods. For example, the design team could decide that 9 points is the minimum for active participation, but levels 4, 5 and 6 must have at least one item with a 4-point value. The previous example actually conforms to this requirement, through the inclusion of site involvement activities at levels 4, 5 and 6. This will ensure Active Participation on a plant level. A visual way to represent the values of Active Participation is with a matrix.

Active Participation Matrix

Scale 1 - 4

	Individual	Team	Department	Site
Team Mtg		2		
Training	1	2	3	4
Cost Mtg		2	3	4
Realibility Mtg		2	3	4
Safety Mtg		2	3	4
Supervisor Fill		2		
Projects	1	2	3	4
Emergency Team		2		
Community Service				4
Hiring Employees				4
Problem Mtg		2	3	4
Certification Board		2	3	4
Others				

Point Values

Exhibit G

Whatever system your team uses, the items chosen should occur naturally to the extent possible in your organization. While I advocate the best method is increased participation at each level, I am sure there are a number of ways you can slice this subject to get a reasonable amount of Active Participation. Keep this process as simple to understand as possible so that it is easily verifiable. You may also want to consider just simply letting the team select the items of Active Participation for each individual. The time has past when an organization can afford to hire an individual who says, "I am just going to give eight hours at a specific job and then go home." Progressive organizations realize that the technicians they hire have much more to give, so ask for it.

Chapter 9

Structuring Levels for Departments and Teams

In the previous chapter, the design team for our hypothetical Company B established the method for assigning point values to each job classification or task area. To recap, here are the criteria for assigning point values:

1. *Time needed to learn technology*   1 week = 5 points
2. *Impact on the business* scale 1 - 20
3. *Decision making*   scale 1 - 15
4. *Environment*   scale 1 - 10
5. *Physical requirements* scale 1 - 10

Next, using these criteria, the design team evaluated three

different task areas found in the plant:

Fork truck operator = *45 points*
Tester = *65 points*
Control room operator = *105 points*

The team determined that a skill set should comprise between 60 and 65 points. The three sample task areas listed above were then compared with this standard. It is evident, the Fork Truck task area would fall short; the Tester task area would comprise one skill set, and the Control Room job is equivalent to almost two skill sets. I intentionally made some of the examples less or more than a skill set, since this is typical of the results you will see in your calibrations.

The following example further illustrates this system as applied to the job classifications found in a typical industrial plant. This work structure can apply to most industrial complexes, whether your industry is textiles, chemicals, wood products, paper, plastics, steel or any other that involves different skills. Included in here are only the operational job classifications. Examples of the maintenance job classifications and the different ways they can be worked into the system will be addressed later in the text.

Operational task areas	Point values
Turbine helper	*15*
Press field operator	*20*
Finished product helper	*25*
Finished product operator	*35*
Fork truck operator	*45*
Turbine operator	*48*
Chemical operator	*60*
Press control operator	*60*
Raw product operator	*60*
Tester	*65*
Control room operator	*60*
Control field	60

Point values have been given to each of these job classifications following the same procedure used in the original three examples. Of course, this was painless for me, but it will not be so for the typical design team. However, let's say for sake of this example that the Company B design team came to consensus on the point values listed above. Now let's go ahead and see how the team will group these task areas into, *Relatively Equal* skill sets for the department. The skill set numbers are arbitrary designations. Your team could instead use letters, codes, or names for the skill sets you develop.

Skill set 1 Tester

Skill set 2 Chemical operator

Skill set 3 Fork truck operator
Press field operator

Skill set 4 Press panel operator

Skill set 5 Finished product operator
Finished product helper

Skill set 6 Turbine operator
Turbine helper

Skill set 7 Control room operator

Skill set 8 Control field

Skill set 9 Raw products operator

Notice that the task areas have been grouped to make the proposed skill sets equal to the standard of between 60 and 65 points per skill set. However, the control room operator task area was evaluated at 105 points. In order to split it into two skill sets (control and field), more technical requirements would have to be added.

When the department teams complete this step, each of the skill sets will have to be presented to the plant design committee for review. This will help to ensure consistency in the calibration process between each of the departments. It is not uncommon for a task area calibration to be either lowered or raised based on a recommendation from the plant design team. This should be a give-and-take process, with constructive feedback aimed at producing a product that will serve the needs of both the plant and the department.

A Modular Approach to Calibration

In the previous example, the task areas were grouped into skill sets in a logical order. By logical order, I mean that the proximity of jobs, or the flow of the process, this is considered along with the timing that is reasonable for employees to acquire successive skill sets. Look at Skill Set 3 (Fork truck operator and Press field operator) and Skill set 5 (Finished product helper and Finished product operator). These two skill sets were put together because of the proximity of equipment, or because of similarity in process. This way of grouping modules has the effect of ensuring more in-depth knowledge in those particular skill areas.

15 technician operational team
Skill Matrix

	1	2	3	4	5	6	7	8	9
Robert	X		X		X	X	X		
Allison			X					X	
Brian	X								X
Francis				X					X
Frank				X			X		
Jim	X			X		X	X		
Bob	X					X			
Art		X	X				X		
Karen				X		X	X		
Sam						X			X
George			X		X				X
Harry				X			X		
Joe	X	X				X			
Sue		X			X			X	
Mary	X	X				X			X

Skill Sets

	1	2	3	4	5	6	7	8	9
Minimum	2	3	2	3	3	4	3	2	4
Maximum	6	9	4	6	6	9	5	7	8

Exhibit H

However, another option can be considered and that is simply looking at the point value for each job evaluated. The tasks can be combined in any manner to make up a full skill set. For example:

Fork truck operator = *45 points*
Turbine helper = *15 points*

Total = *60 points*

A combination approach is also possible. The modular and combination approaches will be discussed in more detail when we consider the maintenance skills.

When the skill sets are matched with the technician that possess them, for each team, a matrix as shown in Exhibit H is developed. These matrices will form a basic tool for managing the team's skill distribution, as well as employee training and career pathing.

Maintenance Skill Sets

As mentioned earlier, the trend throughout industry is to develop multi-craft systems for maintenance-mechanical skills. In multi-craft systems, technicians are expected to perform several different craft areas with proficiency. Over the years, industry has proven that this is a very effective way to develop more skills in the maintenance-mechanical work force. So why change it with the system I am advocating in this book?

Despite the gains made by the multi-craft skills, there is still a need for improved assessment of the value of skills. We need a better method of identifying what skills a specific department needs. There must be a way to select the person most suited for a particular skill area. So how do we get there from here? First we will review the different task areas for which a multi-craft mechanic would be responsible:

- *Shop math*
- *Pneumatics*
- *Hydraulics*
- *Gear reducers*
- *Centrifugal Pumps*
- *Positive displacement pumps*
- *Rigging*
- *Lubrication*
- *Belt drives*
- *Couplings*
- *Chain drives*
- *Alignment*
- *Shop tools*
- *Welding*
- *Welded pipefitting*
- *Screwed pipefitting*

° *Blueprints*
° *Compressors*
° *Screw press*

This list breaks the multi-craft mechanical skills into a number of individual modules. Undoubtedly there are more, and it is also possible to break some of these into smaller components. The next step is to calibrate the mechanical skill modules. I would like to make it clear that I am not suggesting that every individual in your maintenance-mechanical progression has to gain all of these skills. In fact, as I have discussed earlier, that will be up to each person's ability and willingness to contribute, and the availability of skill sets based on the business need of the organization. For this example, we will apply the previous calibration to the skills listed above.

Point Value System

1. Time needed to learn
technology   1 week = 5 points
2. Impact on the business scale 1 - 20
3. Decision making   scale 1 - 15
4. Environment   scale 1 - 10
5. Physical requirements scale 1 - 10

Skill area: Hydraulics

1. Time to train   3 weeks = 15 points
2. Decision making   10 points
3. Impact on business   3 points
4. Environment   5 points
5. Physical demands   2 points
   Total   35 points

Skill area: Shop Tools

1. Time to train   1 week = 5 points
2. Decision making   3 points
3. Impact on business   2 points
4. Environment   3 points
5. Physical demands   2 points
   Total   15 points

Skill area: Blueprint Reading

1. Time to train   1 week = 5 points
2. Decision making   2 points
3. Impact on business   2 points
4. Environment   1 points
5. Physical demands   1 points
   Total   11 points

Skill area: Centrifugal Pumps

1. Time to train   2 weeks = 10 points
2. Decision making   4 points
3. Impact on business   3 points
4. Environment   5 points
5. Physical demands   4 points
   Total   26 points

Skill area: Alignment

1. Time to train   2 weeks = 10 points
2. Decision making   7 points
3. Impact on business   3 points
4. Environment   4 points
5. Physical demands   4 points
   Total   28 points

These examples demonstrate how to apply the calibration tool to mechanical skills. The process is really the same, whether it be operations or maintenance.

Now we will attach a value to the first list so that we can develop some possibilities for skill sets. Again, we have some options on how to develop skill sets. I will present three different possibilities and provide examples of each. Keep in mind that all the mechanical possibilities are not listed; in fact, it would not surprise me to see the typical company calibrate at least twice the number of modules shown.

Shop math	*8*
Pneumatics	*14*
Hydraulics	*35*
Centrifugal pumps	*26*
Gear reducers	*13*
Positive Disp pumps	*20*
Rigging	*10*
Lubrication	*12*
Belt drives	*15*
Couplings	*10*
Chain drives	*15*
Alignment	*28*
Shop tools	*15*
Welding	*45*
Welded pipefitting	*40*
Screwed pipefitting	*15*
Blueprints	*11*
Bearings	*15*
Power tools	*9*
Compressors	*20*
Screwed press	*30*

Using the list, group them into fixed skill sets.

Skill Set 1

Bearings	15 points
Belts	15 points
Chains	15 points
Couplings	10 points
Shop math	8 points
Total	63 points

Skill Set 2

Alignment	28 points
Hydraulics	35 points
Total	63 points

Skill Set 3

Pneumatics	14 points
Positive disp. pumps	20 points
Centrifugal pumps	26 points
Total	60 points

Skill Set 4

Compressors	*35 points*
Shop tools	*15 points*
Rigging	*10 points*
Total	*60 points*

Skill Set 5

Gear reducers	*20 points*
Lubrication	*12 points*
Screwed press	*30 points*
Total	*62 points*

Skill Set 6

Welding	*45 points*
Screwed pipe fitting	*15 points*
Total	*60 points*

Skill Set 7

Welded pipefitting	*40 points*
Blueprints	*11 points*
Power tools	*9 points*
Total	*60 points*

In the above example, each combination of modules equalled one skill set. As with the operational skill sets, the proposed maintenance skill sets will have to be reviewed by the plant design team to determine if the calibration is acceptable.

The seven skill sets developed in this example might be called "fixed" skill sets. By looking at the point value of each of the modules as calibrated by the design team, you can determine what modules each skill set should include. An example of a team matrix with fixed skill sets is shown in Exhibit I.

The fixed skill set is a good method to handle maintenance where there is a natural progression of specific skills that individual technicians can attain. However, this method may not allow sufficient flexibility. For example, a company with a department maintenance structure may wish to allow greater flexibility between departments. If this is the case, the design process could allow each department to determine what goes into the skill sets available to that department.

Fixed Mechanical Skill Set Matrix

12 person Team

	1	2	3	4	5	6	7
Doug	x					x	x
Jack	x	x		x		x	
Sue	x		x	x	x		
Mark	x	x				x	x
Don	x		x		x		
Jim	x	x		x	x		x
Kathy							
Bruce	x		x				
Kevin	x				x		
Sam	x	x		x			x
Karen	x					x	
Joe	x		x	x	x		x
Skill Sets	1	2	3	4	5	6	7
MIN	4	4	3	4	3	2	3
MAX	12	7	5	7	7	5	5

This skill set approach is rigid but it is simple to manage. You must determine if it is flexible enough to produce the business result.

Exhibit I

12 person x 4 skill sets = 48

If a company desires even more flexibility in the system, the design teams can elect to go by the modular approach. The modular approach gives the option of selecting any skill area and combining it with any of others until the required point value is reached that will establish a skill set. Here are a few examples of what modular skill sets could look like:

Modular Skill Set 1

Bearings	*15 points*
Alignment	*28 points*
Gearboxes	*20 points*
Total	*63 points*

Modular Skill Set 2

Blueprint reading	*11 points*
Centrifugal pumps	*31 points*
Pneumatics	*14 points*
Shop math	*8 points*
Total	*64 points*

Modular Skill Set 3

Hydraulics   *35 points*
Screwed press   *30 points*
Total   *65 points*

An example of this type of team matrix is shown in Exhibit J. There can be dozens of different possibilities for a skill set if set up by the modular approach. The advantage of using this approach is it can be customized to meet the needs of the individual and the particular department. As long as the calibration points add up to the 60 to 65 range that we have used in our examples, each would be a skill set.

Module Mechanical Format 12 person team.

module values	8	15	35	26	13	20	10	12	15	10	15	28	15	45	40	15	11	15	9	20	30
	Shop math	Pneumatics	Hydraulics	cent pump	gear	pos pump	Rigging	Lub	Belts	Coupling	chains	Alignment	Shop tools	Welding	Weld pipe	Screw pipe	blueprint	bearings	power tools	compressor	screw press
Doug	x			x		x										x		x		x	
Jack	x	x		x	x						x		x				x				x
Sue	x	x	x		x	x								x				x		x	
Mark	x	x				x	x		x	x			x	x						x	x
Don	x	x	x					x				x	x	x		x		x			
Jim	x	x		x	x		x			x			x	x				x			
Kathy	x										x						x				x
Bruce	x	x						x		x				x	x					x	
Kevin	x	x								x		x						x			
Sam	x	x		x		x		x					x				x	x	x		
Karen	x					x	x		x						x	x				x	
Joe	x		x		x	x	x				x	x	x	x			x			x	x
MIN	72	45	70	78	26	60	50	36	60	50	60	90	60	74	60	60	55	75	45	80	90
MAX	96	60	245	156	65	200	100	96	120	100	120	180	112	240	180	240	180	132	150	108	180

MAX = 65 points X 4 skill sets X 12 persons = 3120 points available

EXHIBIT J

There is a third option when developing maintenance skill sets, is to use a combination approach. With this method, the department design teams have the opportunity to designate certain skill sets they may want all individuals to learn. For example, let's develop some skill sets that are mandatory; that is, all technicians must acquire these skill sets before they can go on and acquire advanced modules.

Mandatory Skill Set 1

Bearings	*15 points*
Belts	*15 points*
Chains	*15 points*
Couplings	*10 points*
Shop math	*8 points*
Total	*63 points*

Mandatory Skill Set 2

Alignment	*28 points*
Hydraulics	*35 points*
Total	*63 points*

Mandatory Skill Set 3

Pneumatics	*14 points*
Centrifugal pumps	*31 points*
Positive disp. pumps	*20 points*
Total	*65 points*

By establishing mandatory skill sets, the teams can ensure that everyone gets the basics of your particular industrial needs from the beginning. Exhibit K is a matrix showing this option for mechanical maintenance.

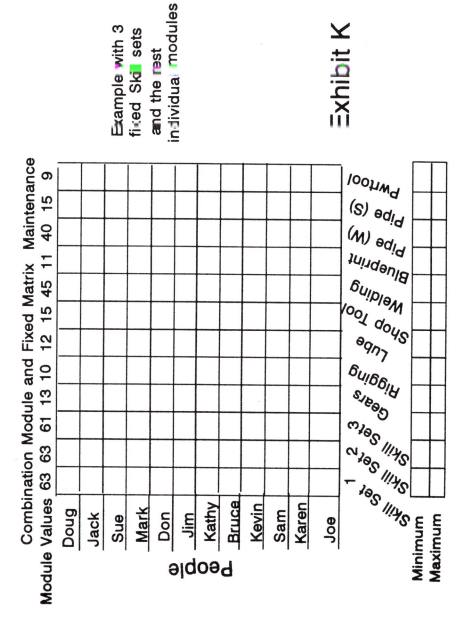

Example with 3 fixed Skill sets and the rest individual modules

Exhibit K

Electrical/Instrumentation Skills

We will now apply some of the same principles to the electrical/instrumentation field as we did to the mechanical skills. The following list of typical electrical/instrumentation skills will be used to work through the examples in this section:

- *Instrumentation safety*
- *Instrumentation theory*
- *Instrumentation diagrams*
- *Instrument calibration*
- *Instrumentation test equipment*
- *Control valve maintenance*
- *Instrumentation troubleshooting*
- *Transmitter maintenance*
- *Programmable logic controllers*
- *Digital theory*
- *Electrical safety*
- *Conduit*
- *Lighting system*
- *Basic electricity*
- *Electrical splicing techniques*
- *Troubleshooting electrical circuits*
- *High voltage maintenance*

Here's the calibration tool again, and this time it is applied to several of the electrical/instrumentation modules:

Point Value System

1. *Time needed to learn technology*   *1 week = 5 points*
2. *Impact on the business   scale 1 - 20*
3. *Decision making   scale 1 - 15*
4. *Environment   scale 1 - 10*
5. *Physical requirements   scale 1 - 10*

Skill area: Instrumentation Theory

1. *Time to train   3 weeks = 15 points*
2. *Decision making   4 points*
3. *Impact on business   6 points*
4. *Environment   1 point*
5. *Physical demands   1 point*
   Total   27 points

Skill area: Electrical Splices

1. Time to train   ½ week = 3 points
2. Decision making   2 points
3. Impact on business   8 points
4. Environment   3 points
5. Physical demands   2 points
    Total   18 points

Skill area: Control Valve Maintenance

1. Time to train   2 week = 10 points
2. Decision making   3 points
3. Impact on business   6 points
4. Environment   2 points
5. Physical demands   2 points
    Total   23 points

Skill area: Digital Theory

1. Time to train   4 weeks = 20 points
2. Decision making   3 points
3. Impact on business   6 points
4. Environment   1 point
5. Physical demands   1 point
    Total   31 points

Now list all the electrical /instrumentation modules from above and attach a calibration value to each:

Instrumentation safety	*6*
Instrumentation theory	*27*
Instr. diagrams	*11*
Instr.calibration	*15*
Instr. test equipment	*22*
Control valve maint.	*23*
Instr. troubleshooting	*23*
Transmitter maint.	*14*
Programmable logic controllers	*40*
Digital theory	*31*
Electrical safety	*6*
Conduit	*12*
Lighting systems	*15*
Basic electricity	*25*
Electrical splicing	*14*
Troubleshooting electrical circuits	*22*
High voltage maint.	*18*

Now that we have the electrical /instrumentation modules calibrated, we can determine the combinations available for this group of skills. First, develop a set skill set pattern:

Skill Set 1

Instrumentation safety	6 points
Electrical safety	6 points
Basic electricity	25 points
Instr. theory	27 points
Total	64 points

Skill Set 2

Instr. diagrams	11 points
Instr. test equipment	22 points
Digital theory	31 points
Total	64 points

Skill Set 3

Instr. calibration	15 points
Instr. transmitter	14 points
Troubleshooting electrical circuits	22 points
Electr. splicing	14 points
Total	65 points

Skill Set 4

Programmable logic controllers	*40 points*
Instr. troubleshooting	*23 points*
Total	*63 points*

Skill Set 5

High voltage maintenance	*22 points*
Lighting systems	*15 points*
Control valve maintenance	*23 points*
Total	*60 points*

This example uses five skill sets; obviously, there are many more that could be developed. I can just hear the electrical-/instrumentation folks saying, these skills are worth twice as many points. Don't panic! You can adapt this system to your specific industrial requirements.

This method uses a fixed progression of skills, with no variation. It makes sense in this discipline, as the learning of electrical/instrumentation skills is very progressive in nature. Developing a matrix for the electrical/instrumentation maintenance team will help to keep track of each individual's contribution to the skills available on the team, as shown in Exhibit L.

Exhibit L

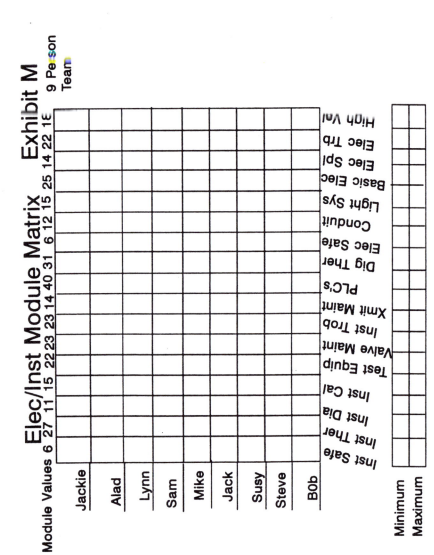

The second method is the modular approach. This allows the different departments to customize a progression pattern for each individual who wants to acquire an electrical/instrumentation skill set. The benefit here is the greater flexibility available to each department when selecting the specific modules needed. The down side is that you must pay special attention to the specific modules that are attained. Shift teams can easily become unbalanced in skills, unless careful attention is paid to career pathing.

By setting up a matrix, the electrical/instrumentation maintenance teams can see at a glance which skills should be acquired next. Exhibit M is an example of this approach.

A third option is to combine the fixed and modular approaches. The design team may want to consider making the first couple of skill sets mandatory to establish the basics of the electrical/instrumentation skill, and then allow the individual technicians to acquire advanced modules based on the business needs. Exhibit N is an example of this approach in matrix form.

Exhibit N

Electrical and Instrumentation — Fixed and Module combination

2 Fixed skill sets plus modules of different values.

9 Person Team

Values	Skill Set 1	Skill Set 2	Inst Cal	Valve Main	Inst Trob	Xmitt Maint	PLC's Conduit	Light Sys	Elec Splice	Elec Trob	High Volt
	64	64	15	23	23	14	40	12	15	14	22	18
Jackie											
Alad											
Lynn											
Sam											
Mike											
Jack											
Susy											
Steve											
Bob											

	Skill Set 1	Skill Set 2	Inst Cal	Valve Main	Inst Trob	Xmitt Maint	PLC's Conduit	Light Sys	Elec Splice	Elec Trob	High Volt
Minimum	576	576	60	92	115	70	80	36	75	56	66	36
Maximum	576	576	135	184	161	112	200	72	90	98	154	72

60x4x9=2160

Skills are Skills

Another feature of a traditional systems in industry is that there have always been some natural divisions that create barriers in the organizational structure. The most common barrier is the adversarial relationship between the operations and maintenance functions. Having experienced both sides in my career in industry, I understand that this relationship is somewhat natural. The two functions have competing priorities, or so it seems. The operational element want to keep the equipment up and running as long as possible, while the maintenance element wants to preform regularly scheduled maintenance to avoid a catastrophic failure that will cost more down time in the long run. It seems that never do the two sides meet at a happy medium. This is not to say that the dispute is unresolved, but the understanding never seems to be quite there on either side.

One way to modify this naturally adversarial relationship is to integrate maintenance and operational skills. A high performance work structure can do this. After all, when you hire a person who is willing and able but needs specific training for your industry, you have not labeled that person with either the maintenance or the operational banner. Designing a high performance work structure enables you to designate skill areas needed on any given team that combine operational and maintenance skill set availability. The business will benefit, since now you will have technicians on teams that will have a thorough understanding of good maintenance practices, and can use their operational skills to troubleshoot a potential or real problem. This allows the technician to become a more versatile contributor.

As you follow the process described in this book, be open minded when you make skill sets available for each team and department. Blending skills will increase both the employee's and the departments flexibility in amazing ways. This gets rid of the I-can only perform-one-or-the-other syndrome. What would you call a person who could give your organization both operational and maintenance skills, besides valuable? This person has more claim to the title Technician than anyone else who has just maintenance or operational skills. The operations vs. maintenance adversarial relationship, is one of the hardest relationships to break, and that is because it has been imbedded in industry for so long. If you make the skills available through your design, this mind set will eventually fade away.

Let's take a look at an example of a team matrix that has both operational and maintenance skills available to all of the team members. Exhibit O is an example of this approach. Remember, this does not have to be a force fit, it is simply a number of skill sets that are available to that team. I have seen the potential of blending these skills and it should not be ignored, it again sends the message of what the organization values in its employees.

15 technician team Skill Matrix
Blending Operational and Maintenance | Maint

Skill Sets →	1	2	3	4	5	6	7	8	9	10	11	12
Robert	X			X		X	X					
Allison			X					X				
Brian	X											
Francis				X					X			
Frank					X			X				
Jim	X									X	X	X
Bob	X					X						
Art		X	X					X				
Karen				X		X	X					
Sam						X			X			
George			X	X	X				X			
Harry				X			X					
Joe	X	X				X						
Sue		X			X			X				
Mary	X	X				X			X			
Minimum	2	3	2	3	3	4	3	2	4	2	2	2
Maximum	6	6	4	6	6	7	5	7	6	3	3	3

Exhibit O

Whichever method your team chooses, it is vital to monitor closely the modules needed for business purposes. As in the operational skill set examples, we must remember the economic needs of the business. Therefore we must establish the minimum and maximum number of skill sets and/or modules technicians are expected to acquire. This can be based (for example) on an average of four skill sets per technician. We will incorporate this minimum and maximum availability into the matrix so that, as we plan career pathing for the individual technicians, we can be assured to obtain the skill sets or modules that are required on the team.

Skill Set Availability

At this point, the department teams are proceeding with the process of developing the skill sets. The next step in the process is to establish the minimum number of technicians who will have each of the particular skill sets.

Why should we even be concerned with minimums? Didn't I tell you that you would have at least twice as many skills now as you did in a traditional system?

Since the technicians are going to have a lot of skill sets after the transition, why be concerned with the minimums?

The company must manage the availability of skills: not because there will be more of them, but because *improper distribution of skills can create problems for teams.* Think about how many persons with each skill set you absolutely must have to cover vacation, training and absenteeism. Isn't that similar to the way you tried to cover the necessary skills in a traditional system? This is why it is called *"minimum available skill sets."*

When developing minimum availability, the design team should consult with supervisors for input in this particular area. The supervisors know (or should know) what is needed, at a minimum, to keep the operation running. After you determine which skill sets the team needs, at a minimum, and after it is determined which of the technicians has which of the skill sets in the new system, it will be necessary to have a good measuring tool to make sure that:

(1) the distribution of skill sets is balanced on the team, and

(2) each skill set is represented by at least the minimum number of technicians possessing that skill set.

Again, a good way to do this is with a matrix. Using the skill sets we developed earlier, here is look at a sample for a team consisting of fifteen technicians:

Minimum Skill Set Availability
15 Technicians on Team

Skill set 1	2 technicians
Skill set 2	3 technicians
Skill set 3	2 technicians
Skill set 4	3 technicians
Skill set 5	3 technicians
Skill set 6	4 technicians
Skill set 7	3 technicians
Skill set 8	2 technicians
Skill set 9	4 Technicians

Total 26 skill sets

Use this method to set standards for the minimum number of skill sets available on each team. Be sure to consider absenteeism, vacation time, training, etc.

Maximum Skill Set Availability

In an existing facility, the minimum skill set availability should, for the most part, be met as a result of the skill development that has already occurred through the traditional progression. The next step is to determine the maximum skill set availability. This has two purposes.

First, remember one of the requirements for the new system is that it must be economically feasible. It is a business, and pricing yourself out of business is not an option. So how do you go about making sure it is feasible? You simply determine the average straight time rate that makes the program economically practical. This is the rate that will be attached to each pay level, or level of skill attained.

For example, using four levels of pay as the mark to make the work structure economically feasible. Take this information and use it to determine the skill set availability per team. Using the same fifteen technician team for purposes of this example, we have:

15 technicians x an average of 4 levels = 60 skill sets

Now we have the maximum number of skill sets available. Here is an example of how the maximum might be distributed among the various skill sets:

Maximum Skill Set Availability
15 Technicians on Team

Skill set 1	6 technicians
Skill set 2	9 technicians
Skill set 3	4 technicians
Skill set 4	6 technicians
Skill set 5	6 technicians
Skill set 6	9 technicians
Skill set 7	5 technicians
Skill set 8	7 technicians
Skill set 9	8 technicians

Total 60 skill sets

The second reason to address maximum skill set availability is balance. Again, look at the team matrix. The matrix will show which skill sets are filled and which ones are short. Without some method to spread the skill sets around among the team members, the more popular skill sets would be the place where the technicians would gravitate. When we discuss career pathing for technicians in the next chapter, we will look at the matrix again to examine the implications it will have for the individual. Refer to Exhibit H to see minimums and maximums on the Skills Matrix.

Part 4

Making The Transition to High Performance

Chapter 10

From Old to New Making the Transition

The plant design team has developed the major components of the high performance work structure. The department design teams have added the detail to the umbrella. A new work system is defined for the plant. Now what do you do?

The next important step to find a fair way to evaluate the skills of the technicians within the framework of the high performance work structure. The criteria developed here should be temporary in nature. Therefore, one of the first guidelines the plant should establish is how long to complete the transition from the old pay structure to the new. Even though this new work structure is designed to accomplish long-term gains, the transition should be completed as soon as possible.

For a union plant, I would suggest that the best time is to begin the transition is in conjunction with contract negotiation time. You probably will have little choice, but it's the right time anyway.

It has been my experience, the optimum transition time should be no more than a year. Why a year? Because the plant is faced with the task of evaluating the skill sets that people actually have, whether or not they have been asked to use them. Naturally, since you expect more from the technician there must be *gains* for the technician.

Setting Pay Rates for Levels

The management team should have already evaluated the skills the typical employee has under the traditional progression that has occurred. Remember, each employee has usually gone through several job classifications, depending on how long they have been with the company. Thus, the company often has data that can be used to make some assessments. A typical pay scale for technicians might look like the following:
(note: this is mid range scale your industry may be higher or lower)

Traditional Pay Rate (average rate for years of service)

technicians	2 years	8.50
technicians	6 years	9.00
technicians	10 years	10.25
technicians	14 years	11.00
technicians	18 years	11.75
technicians	22 years	12.50
technicians	26 years	13.75

Such data can be utilized to determine the appropriate pay rate per level under the new system. A comparison is made between the amount of time (under the old system) that equates to each of the skill sets that have been developed.

You might think the assessment could just as easily have been done first place. It could have, but it is not really necessary as one of your principles is that it has to be cost effective. You also need to know the numbers of levels and the relationship of skills to the levels to attach pay so you might as well leave this for last. If you don't it will influence some of the other skill set decisions unnecessarily. For sure the people working on the design of the system do not need to be bothered with this, they have a big enough task. Fear not, it will work out.

Now the plant needs to do a department-by-department general assessment, based on the skill sets in each department. This can be done primarily by the supervisors, and reviewed by the department managers. They will understand what skill sets each individual on their team will likely be able to attain within the one year transition time.

Here is such an assessment for one department:

Assessment Prior to Transition
(15 - technician team)

2 technicians   *2 years*   *2 = 1 skill set*

3 technicians   *6 years*   *3 = 2 skill sets*

3 technicians   *10 years*   *3 = 3 skill sets*

3 technicians   *14 years*   *1 = 3 skill sets*
                                2 = 4 skill sets

2 technicians   *18 years*   *2 = 4 skill sets*

1 technician   *22 years*   *1 = 5 skill sets*

1 technician   26 years   1 = 5 skill sets

Of course, each company will have its own data, but this is a typical example. The exact distribution will depend on the length of time your work force has been employed and the turnover rate in your industry.

To continue on with this example, examine your company's data to determine what the employees have been paid for a given amount of time on the job. Now consider the department-by-department evaluation of where the skill sets will probably end. With this information, proceed to establish pay rates. Remember, there must be something in it for the technician, and there must be something in it for the company.

Look at an example that illustrates one obvious benefit to the technician who is able and willing to contribute to the success of the organization under the high performance work structure:

High Performance Work Structure

pay rate

Level	1	9.00
Level	2	9.75
Level	3	10.75
Level	4	12.50

| Level | 5 | 14.75 |
| Level | 6 | 16.00 |

Understand that the numbers given are just an example. The pay rates selected for this example are probably in the mid range if you considered industry as a whole.

There are a couple of items to note regarding the pay rates as shown above. The first is to review what employees were making under the traditional, as in the example at the beginning of this chapter. By comparison, changing over to the new system should equate to more *money* for the employee. Give the technician a reason for wanting to go through with the transition!

The second point to remember is that the pay rate goes up in an exponential manner. The reasoning for this is as a technician acquires additional skill sets, that person has more skills to maintain than those with fewer skill sets. Therefore equal pay increments do not reflect the additional effort required to acquire and maintain each additional skill set. This is a minor point, but remember everything you do in your design of a high performance work structure *sends a message*, so search for any opportunity to send the right message.

Now you have established a pay schedule for the levels in your new system. That pay schedule gives the technician one good reason to move into the new structure. The next reason has to be that your plant has established a time period for the conversion. I suggested a year, but do not go over two years, go ahead and get on with the new program!

When the company begins the process of implementing a high performance work structure, it must develop a procedure for the evaluation of technical skills. I would suggest one overall policy for these evaluations: *Until the transition is complete, limit the number of skill sets an individual technician can have to that which is no more than one level above the current pay system.* In other words, do not initially allow any individual to jump to a two-level pay change. There are several reasons for this. You will have a lot of evaluations to perform, and you have a commitment to evaluate all the technicians in your department. The one-level policy provides opportunities for a pay raise initially, and those technicians who do have the additional skill sets can go through the permanent procedure that will be set up for new skill sets after the transition. In any case, those individuals who say they have more than one additional level of skill sets will be the exceptions. This policy will save your company some grief during the transition.

Regarding the actual process of evaluating technicians' skills, one way is to use this approach:

First, set up a department team to meet with each individual technician. Allow the individual to petition the department team with the skill sets that they believe they have.

Second, allow the technicians to demonstrate they have

the skills by performing the task areas defined in the skill sets. The essential elements of the skill sets should already be documented. Assign your most qualified technicians in that skill set to help with the evaluations of that area. Employees who have worked extensively in a particular skill area are normally well-suited to conduct these reviews. Have the shift supervisor and the senior technician perform an oral examination of the evaluated technician's skill, and observe the actual job performance.

This will accomplish a couple of things for your system: It will establish the fact that you are actually going to require use of the skills in the skill sets the technician is claiming. Second, you can be assured of performance before you allow that individual to perform the skill set without supervision. This procedure is also less threatening to the technician than a certification review board that is totally concerned with questions and answers.

What else do you need to evaluate to complete the conversion to the new structure? Bet you forgot about Active Participation. Remember, the system includes more than just technical skills. Do not make the mistake of changing over without considering all the requirements that the plant design team recommended. Remember Active Participation is an ingredient that gives the organization more potential from the technician.

Documentation of this component is very important. Document specifically what that person claims for the point value of that specific skill set. Refer back to the section and check the requirements for Active Participation. Remember, the items that were detailed have natural amounts of participation, so get what you ask for in this area.

The department transition team reviews each technician's active participation along with technical skills prior to allowing the pay raise. This participation will set your organization apart and make it different and better for the effort.

There are other ways to accomplish the transition. If you chose, you could use an oral evaluation of the skill sets in which an individual claims proficiency. With this method, you must rely on the supervisor's assessment of the technician's ability to perform a previously acquired skill. This is an easier method, but it would not be my first choice. Remember the message, and make sure you are not just giving lip service to the expectation of utilizing all the skills attained.

Other Transition Questions

What happens at the end of the transition period to those individuals who have not made the effort to be evaluated? This question should be answered before beginning the transition. People should always know the consequences of their actions, including non-compliance with work rules.

There will always be some individuals in the category of the "able but unwilling." You have several options, but before we get to them, it is important to work individually with the technicians to help them make transition.

Send the message that the company wants to give credit where credit is due. Develop a plan for each individual on each team. When a few individuals attain the additional pay that comes with the new system, you will see a growth in momentum to help speed the transition.

The "able but unwilling" employees will be the exception, not the norm. Therefore, the person who refuses to comply should, at the end of the transition period, be paid at whatever level they are performing. Obviously, if they have not gone through an oral or technical review or generated any evidence of active participation, entry level pay would seem appropriate. This may sound harsh, but again you did not want this confrontation issue. Think about the message! If you do nothing, there is no reason for anybody to believe you are serious. What about the technician who comes up short in the evaluation process? This is one of the reasons you should allow a year for the transition. These technicians retain their old pay rate until they are able to demonstrate the required proficiency. This is also why it does not pay to procrastinate about making the transition.

What is the possibility of losing people because of the work structure change? It will happen, and when it occurs it will be for a couple of different circumstances. The first is the person who is a very long-term employee and about ready to retire, but is unwilling to cope with a traumatic event of a change. Change seems to affect the long term employee more because they tend to be set in a particular pattern. This will only affect a few people in your organization. Remember your transition plan helps by giving the employee a reason to get on with the new system.

The second loss of personnel will occur with those who are simply unwilling to change, unwilling to contribute more to the organization. In my experience with various companies, this type of personnel loss is usually minimal. Occasionally you may also lose a supervisor who does not agree with the new work structure philosophy.

It would be easy to ignore the possibility of losing some personnel, but if your plan has to please everyone you had better not even start the process of change. Remember, the reason you are in business is to make a product as effectively as possible. The reason for making this change is to utilize the human resource in a more effective way.

Chapter 11

Training and Career Pathing for the New System

In an existing business in a traditional environment, determining training availability is fairly simple. When a job vacancy occurs, someone is selected for that vacancy and starts training. In a high performance work structure there is more opportunity for obtaining skills and achieving a promotion. However, many people in high performance organization have the mistaken impression that all skills are available to an employee simply based on that individual's desire to learn and demonstrate the skill area. However, in the real world there are other important considerations:

How many technicians can train at one time without interruption to the business of making a product?

In order to answer this, you will need some additional information. First, how much extra staffing is needed to cover for employees who are in training? You have obviously addressed this question to some extent, since the domino effect of filling vacancies has mandated training in the old system.

In the new system, the management of each department will decide the appropriate number of training slots to make available. Depending on the structure you already have, your training policy may require very little change. This is because in an existing organization, which is what we are talking about now, many of the skills that will be included in the skill sets are already there, you just have not asked for them to be utilized.

Do not confuse the transition from the old system to the high performance work structure with a training program for learning new skills. In the transition from old to new, the evaluation of skills not used will and should take place to allow technicians credit for those skills. This should require minimal additional training, or a certification process of those prior skills.

It is absolutely imperative to develop a plan specifying how many people can train at any one time. For example, with a 15-technician crew you should be able to allow training for 3 to 5 persons at any one time. You could set a percentage for the plant, say between 20 and 33 percent. This policy will allow the teams to add new skills at a reasonable rate, and it will not disrupt the business of making a product.

When considering the question of how many people can train at one time, remember that in most traditional organizations there is a job classification called Utility. This classification will be unnecessary in a high performance work structure, because more individuals will have the flexibility to perform multiple job tasks. The Utility person, when considered in your staffing plans, now provides a way to free up other people for training opportunities.

Now that we have discussed training opportunities, here is a sample policy for a department. I recommend that the development of training policy be handled on a department-by-department basis. This will allow for greater flexibility from one department to another, and possibly allow for more training opportunities overall.

A typical sequence of training in the department:

1. Testing (written/oral) for knowledge
2. On the job training, fully supervised with trainer
3. On the job training, unsupervised

This sequence is fairly general, and applies to most industrial situations. Obviously it could be more detailed, but for this example we will use the generic version:

Department Training Policy
15 - person team

1. *No more than 10 percent overtime per month allowed per technician in training.*

2. *No more than 3 technicians in fully supervised training per 15-person team.*

3. *No more than 5 technicians total in unsupervised and fully-supervised training per 15 technician team.*

4. *When people are out for whatever reason, supervised training is reduced by that amount of absenteeism.*

Statement one would control your overtime due to training requirements, but would allow time to work on training with other shift or day teams. It also allows technicians to accomplish some of the individual work, such as testing, on their own.

Statement two would limit the number of senior technicians devoting full time to help with the training activity.

Statement three would allow some technicians to continue to refine their skills until they are ready to be certified in the skill set. Be sure to set a time period for the technician to complete training. If you do not, it will affect the opportunity of others to train, and thus limit their progress to promotion.

Statement four will allow you to plan for when technicians are absent. This will ensure that training does not take precedence over production of the product.

Who gets to train next?

The traditional way to determine which employee gets the next training opportunity is to handle it by seniority. Will this way work? Sure; it does have the benefit of being simple. Is it the best way? If you remember the discussion about treating people fairly rather than "the same," you will realize that just because an employee has been there the longest does not mean that he or she is the best person for that particular skill set.

One of the good things about the high performance work

structure is that the career path is designed to address the right skill set for each individual. So, you will need another set of criteria to determine which employee trains next. What should you consider?

1. *Performance evaluations for other skill sets*
2. *Attendance*
3. *Safety record*
4. *Time it took to gain previous skill set*
5. *Team recommendation based upon who applied to train*
6. *Business need for that particular skill set*
7. *Initiative*
8. *Amount of active participation in work structure*
9. *Demonstrated ability to train others*

These items should be used as a starting point to develop a different kind of selection process other than the traditional seniority method. If you cannot get completely away from the seniority principle, it won't be a disaster. But you should consider the possibility of determining who deserves to train next without the context of seniority. This is about treating people fairly, not "equally."

If you are dealing with a new plant, seniority will not be an issue. Now you have the opportunity to develop criteria for training selection based on performance. A training policy is essential, whether you have an existing plant or a new one. Make sure you control the work structure, instead of the work structure controlling you.

Certification and Documentation

Everyone who accomplishes a goal in life wants to feel that it has value, not only in the eyes of the achiever, but also by the people important to them. Since this is true, what are the important elements in a certification process? You will find they are the same things we have been discussing throughout this book:

° Fairness
° Consistency
° Equality of assessment

In addition to determining if a technician has accomplished the skills your system requires for progression to the next level, a process should be developed to inspect the result. Remember, you get what you inspect! Everyone in your organization must know that the certification process has integrity. It must be perceived as fair, and all technicians applying for a specific skill set must be treated equally.

Let's talk about equality. Throughout this book, I have stressed that people are not equal and this fact has to be recognized. However, as a technician proceeds to gain a pay level in any skill set, the amount of effort it takes to gain the skill must be as equal from one technician to another as possible.

There is something about the written word that gives a process more validity. Do you remember a time when you received a certificate of achievement? That put the stamp of approval on your accomplishment. Documentation is important because it gives that stamp of approval to the promotion process.

In order to determine what documentation is necessary in a high performance work structure, look at the component parts of a skill set. Any one of your skill sets will do; the detail is the only part that would be affected. As discussed previously, the component parts of any skill set are:

° Technical Skill
° Active Participation

Both of these component parts must be verified in the documentation process. Active participation is an expectation in your system, so inspect for it.

Keep the documentation for the review process as simple as possible. Complicating the documentation requirements, for the most part, will just create another opportunity for technicians to complain that they will not go before a certification board because this part of the process is too cumbersome. Active participation, for example, can be recorded on a one-page document, with the technician obtaining signatures in the specific areas of activities claimed. The documentation that you develop for each area that you should inspect (training, active participation, certification review) will add credibility to your system.

Documentation for the technical skill segment of the certification process will be the most detailed. The component parts of the technical skill certification may be broken down into several distinct elements:

1. *Testing (oral or written)*
2. *Demonstrating*
3. *Communicating*

The first step should be to review the technical skill information that includes the safety considerations as well as all the process issues that need to be known prior to actually doing the task in the field. The amount of education your work force has will determine whether or not a written test is appropriate. A written test will always be perceived by the technicians as the least subjective method.

When several people give oral examinations on a one-to--one basis, there is a tendency toward inconsistent results. So, if at this first stage it is necessary to give an oral examination, have several people administer it, and then determine the results by consensus. One possible makeup of the testing group would be a shift supervisor and two other technicians who have solid knowledge of the skill set.

Throughout this process, document the results of successful testing, and pay special attention to what the technician needs to work on before preceding to the next step. Written testing is preferred in these cases because it lends itself to equality of material and consistency. Develop your testing to ask questions that cannot be answered by simple memorization, but require an understanding of the technical process.

Demonstration

This will be the most time-consuming part of the process. This is where the task analysis comes into the picture. Most organizations know and have documented all the individual elements of a particular skill. Each element that has to be performed should be performed enough times so that the examiner or trainer is confident that the skill can be accomplished proficiently without additional help. The technician you designate as a trainer must be able put their name on the line. The documentation has to be developed in such a way that the trainer signs off on each specific demonstrated skill. Furthermore, both the trainee and the trainer need work as a team through this process. You want to avoid the pitfall that comes if both individuals are not held accountable for results.

I realize that for some skills the training process may require several persons to be involved in monitoring the demonstration of these skill areas. However, you should still consider having one technician responsible for the overall training.

Certification Board

Once the training portion is completed, the technician is ready to go before the certification review board. The reason you have a certification board is to make sure employees receive a fair and consistent review of the process. In most cases, the function of the certification board is simply to affirm that all the steps have been taken, and that the technician really understands the technical elements of the skill set.

The certification review process needs to be developed at least at the department level, and at the site level if applicable. Doing this at the department level lends consistency to all the teams. The certification review board should consist of peers and managers who are not on the technician's shift team, and who are familiar with the skill set. The board should accept or reject the technician's certification *by consensus*, and the results should be documented.

An element that has caused trouble with the certification review process occurs when the boards do not allot a specific amount of time for the review. Setting a time limit gives consistency to the review process and forces the board to be more structured. It also gives employees the perception of equal treatment by each board. Try to limit the review process to as short a period as possible; one hour or two hours is often sufficient.

There are some technicians who will say, "I can do it in the field so you should not test me." With very few exceptions, I have found that if a person cannot explain the way to accomplish a process, that person is doing the process incorrectly. Do not accept "I can do it in the field" unless you are willing to lower your standards! Your certification board may have to make some concessions by going out to watch the demonstration again at the certification process. Just make sure you are getting what you are asking for. If a technician cannot communicate the critical elements of a skill set, do you want that technician to train the next one?

Career Pathing/Planning

Now it's time to use the tools your plant design team and department design teams have developed to produce a more effective career pathing system. As an individual in the high performance work structure what do I need to look for to obtain a promotion? Let's look at the considerations about what skill sets will be available. The method that we previously went through to develop the skill sets allowed us to develop a matrix of skills for the particular department and team involved in the career pathing process.

The process of career pathing has two elements. The first and the most important is the business need; that is, which specific skill is necessary to enable the business to move forward as a result of an effort by the individual performing the skill area? The second element involves working with the individual and the team to accommodate the technician's desire to perform in a specific skill set.

Obviously this system offers many choices for the individual and for the company, so variety should not be a problem. Within the framework of team dynamics, you have two options on how to select individuals for training:

° **First option:** *The whole team can become involved in deciding in which skill set a specific individual should begin training.*

° **Second option:** *The team supervisor and the individual study the team's matrix and make the appropriate decision.*

In either option, as long as employees have a common understanding of the high performance work structure and are guided by the team's matrix, the decision process will work appropriately.

There is, however, a warning that must be stated in regard to career pathing: *Only consider the next immediately available training slot for each individual.* There is often a tendency to try to map out the next several skill areas for the individual. In reality, the only time you know when an individual is going to train is when the slot that individual has been allocated. If you were to prematurely allocate two or three additional skill sets, and then went on to allocate one of those to another technician, the first person might be concerned that you are giving away *"their"* skill sets.

In fact, the only skill sets that should "belong" to an individual are the ones that they are certified in, and possibly the one they are currently training in. Remember, fortune telling does not work well when trying to determine an individual's capability. People you think will continue to progress will stop, while people you think will stop will continue to learn and contribute at higher levels. Let it happen; the company will become the beneficiary.

When a training opportunity becomes available, then and only then, a team has the opportunity to determine two things:

1. *What skill set does the team need for business purposes?*
2. *Which technician will be selected for the opportunity to train?*

What happens when the team decides upon a skill set, and the individual who is selected for training does not want that particular skill set? If that happens, you can simply go to the next individual in the selection process — but what if none of them want it? Then keep the training slot open and let the next new employee train for that skill set.

This brings us to another point to discuss before we get into career pathing. The new employee is at the mercy of the team to which he or she is assigned. The team or the supervisor will determine which skill set the individual will train for as a result of business needs. Therefore, *hiring people for specific jobs is no longer necessary.* Instead, you should hire people who have the capability of learning and who are willing and able to contribute.

Here are a couple of scenarios for career pathing in an operational team. In order to develop the scenario, let's take another look at the operational team matrix that we developed earlier. In Exhibit L, we find the same matrix with the minimum and maximum added for each skill set.

The operational team has a training opportunity and, using the criteria established by the department, has selected Brian to be the person given the opportunity. Everyone on the team has studied the matrix and determined which skill set is logical for the team to acquire next.

Let's ask Brian what skill set he would like to train for, and see if we can accommodate both the business needs and Brian's preference. Brian has requested to train in the following skill sets, in order of his preference:

1: *Skill set 2*
2: *Skill set 4*
3: *Skill set 5*

15 technician operational team
Skill Matrix   Exhibit P

	skill set 1	skill set 2	skill set 3	skill set 4	skill set 5	skill set 6	skill set 7	skill set 8	skill set 9
Robert	X			X		X	X		
Allison		X	X					X	
Brian	X								X
Francis				X					X
Frank					X	X	X	X	
Jim	X			X		X	X		
Bob	X					X	X		
Art		X	X						
Karen				X		X	X	X	
Sam						X			X
George			X	X	X				X
Harry							X		
Joe	X	X			X	X			
Sue	X	X						X	
Mary		X				X			X
Minimum	2	3	2	3	3	4	3	2	4
Maximum	6	9	4	6	6	9	5	7	8

In order to make a good decision, we should look at the distribution of all skill sets shown in the operational matrix :

Skill set 1 Criteria 2 minimum / 6 maximum
  • 6 technicians now have the skill set

Skill set 2 Criteria 3 minimum / 9 maximum
  • 4 technicians now have the skill set

Skill set 3 Criteria 2 minimum / 4 maximum
  • 4 technicians now have the skill set

Skill set 4 Criteria 3 minimum / 6 maximum
  • 4 technicians now have the skill set

Skill set 5 Criteria 3 minimum / 6 maximum
  • 4 technicians now have the skill set

Skill set 6 Criteria 4 minimum / 9 maximum
  • 7 technicians now have the skill set

Skill set 7 Criteria 3 minimum / 5 maximum
  • 4 technicians now have the skill set

Skill set 8 Criteria 2 minimum / 7 maximum
  4 technicians now have the skill set

Skill set 9 Criteria   4 minimum / 8 maximum
   5 technicians now have the skill set

According to this information, skill sets 1 and 3 are at the maximum and therefore are not available. Remember Brian has skill sets 1 and 9.

By looking at the Matrix it shows:

- *Skill set 1 has 0 openings*
- *Skill set 2 has 3 openings*
- *Skill set 3 has 0 openings*
- *Skill set 4 has 2 openings*
- *Skill set 5 has 2 openings*
- *Skill set 6 has 2 openings*
- *Skill set 7 has 1 openings*
- *Skill set 8 has 3 openings*
- *Skill set 9 has 3 openings*

With this information, the team determines that Brian will be able to train for Skill set 2, which is his first choice.

It's good when it works out for both the business and for

the individual. Wouldn't it be nice if that happened all the time in real life? Now let's look at an example that may not be so clear. In order to create a new scenario, let's make a few changes to the same operational team matrix (see exhibit Q) by assuming that, for Skill set 9, there are only 4 technicians with that particular skill set. This means that the team is operating at the minimum acceptable level for that skill set. Therefore, the next skill set that the team needs to acquire is Skill set 9. If this does not fit with the technician selected to train preferences, and that technician does not decide to take the slot another technician will be offered the training opportunity. Remember, business needs first, personal preference second and when the two coincide that's all the better.

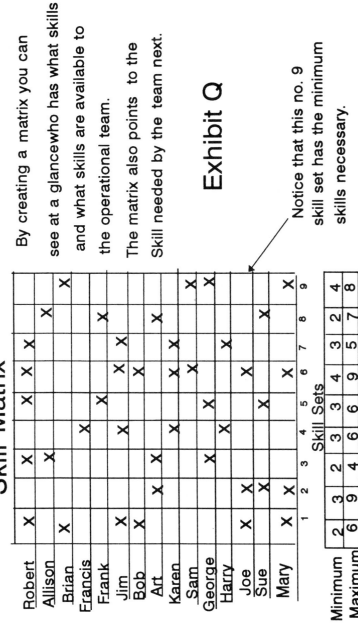

15 technician operational team
Skill Matrix

	1	2	3	4	5	6	7	8	9
Robert	X				X	X	X		
Allison			X					X	
Brian	X								X
Francis				X					
Frank					X			X	
Jim	X			X		X	X		
Bob	X					X	X		
Art		X	X					X	
Karen				X	X	X	X		
Sam							X		X
George			X		X				X
Harry				X	X			X	
Joe	X	X				X			
Sue		X			X			X	
Mary	X	X				X			X

	1	2	3	4	5	6	7	8	9
Minimum	2	3	2	3	3	4	3	2	4
Maximum	6	9	4	6	6	9	5	7	8

Skill Sets

By creating a matrix you can see at a glance who has what skills and what skills are available to the operational team.

The matrix also points to the Skill needed by the team next.

Exhibit Q

Notice that this no. 9 skill set has the minimum skills necessary.

The Matrix as a tool has been discussed at length, it is designed to be a visual representation of the values of your organization. The matrix used in the manner that I have described will give a single tool that the Plant Manager to the Technician can use to give the following information:

- *Shows technical skills needed for department/plant*

- *Gives the value of different skills*

- *Shows department skill availability*

- *Shows team skill availability*

- *Shows individual skill acquisition*

- *Shows what skill needs to be acquired next*

- *Shows if the team/department has a balance of skills*

- *Controls the cost of the system*

- *Sets the minimum acceptable skill level for team/department*

- *Sets the maximum skill availability for each skill set*

- *Allows each department/plant to customize skill needs*

This type of information is invaluable. It sends the message about what a company values. When a training opportunity becomes available, it really makes the decision-making process easy. This work structure is designed to make proper business decisions and take into consideration the individual's preference for career pathing. Remember, the person should have the option to either accept the training opportunity, or reject it and allow someone else to train in that particular skill.

Why is it important to allow a person to reject a particular skill set? We all know that, in life, we have to do certain things because we have no choice — like pay taxes and die. If we increase the opportunity for choice in the work place, it is more likely that a person will try to do a better job at acquiring the skill. So, if possible, let there be choice. This type of career pathing makes many combinations and choices possible, and this will allow greater flexibility that will enhance business results.

Take a look at Matrix exhibit P so we can see which skill sets Robert has acquired.

Skill set	1	Tester
Skill set	3	Fork truck/Press field
Skill set	5	Finished product oper/helper
Skill set	6	Turbine operator/helper
Skill set	7	Control room operator

Looking at exhibit R you will notice an inverted triangle. At each level, I repeated the previous skills acquired. This representation is intended to reenforce a principle that was stated earlier in the text. *Pay for knowledge without utilization gives little or no value to your organization.* If a technician obtains a skill set, they should maintain the technical knowledge required to keep current in that skill set. They should at some frequency utilize that knowledge to enhance the business results of the organization.

Individual Career Path
Technican with 5 Skill sets

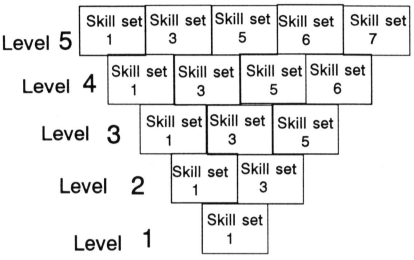

Skill set 1 = Tester

Skill set 3 = Fork truck operator
Press field operator

Skill set 5 = Finished product oper
Finished product helper

Skill set 6 = Turbine operator
Turbine helper

Skill set 7 = Control room operator

Technican Robert

Exhibit R

It is tempting to say that it would be an expectation that each skill area a technician is certified in must get equal time from that technician when it comes to utilization. This interpretation of utilization would be more rigid than necessary. Utilization can occur when that person is utilized as a trainer, or works on that particular skill set in overtime, or of course in the normal course of a work day. Your organization may want to set a minimum time the technician must spend in each skill set area. That minimum amount of time should be enough so you are sure if and when asked to perform that skill set, that it will be performed proficiently. A word of warning, you need to inspect to make sure this occurs. *Remember, you don't always get what you expect, but you get what you inspect.* Just simply have the supervisor/team leader include this aspect in their monthly report.

Summary

Are you sending the message you want your work force to hear? I'm asking you to think about the talent you know exists in your organization. By design you have the opportunity to let the individuals in your organization tell you what they are able and willing to contribute. By design you can compensate the people based on overall contribution to your organization. In Industry both for management and unions, it has been the easy method to treat everyone the "same", even though we know they are not. If the reason that work structures have not changed over the years has been because of mistrust or simplicity, neither answer is acceptable.

Looking for ways to be more competitive is what will keep industry strong. If you believe the status quo will take you into the future, take a good look around. Industry is dealing in a global economy and in order to compete we must do the things that make our industries world class. Your competitors are looking for ways to take advantage of your inflexibility. Let's get out of the syndrome of treating everyone the same. By design it is possible to treat people fairly based on your values, expressed in your promotion structure.

Everybody wins!

Glossary

Active Participation - Those items that a technician can do to further the business with other than technical skills, such as leadership, community involvement and soft skills.

Business Needs - A decision based on the following factors: Safety - Productivity - Quality

Calibration - The exercise of determining the technical value of each of the tasks in your organization.

Career Pathing/Planning - The process of determining the right technical skill set a technician should acquire next.

Contribution - The amount of technical and active participation a technician provides to the organization.

Corporate Direction - General value statement that reflects the corporate values.

Department - A division of your business that takes care of one segment of the business.

Design Team (plant) - A group that develops the general components of the design that applies to the entire plant.

Design Team (department) - The group within the specific department that adds the detail as it pertains to that specific department.

Level - A level of pay corresponding to the amount of contribution a technician provides to the organization.

Maintain - To keep current with the technical requirements of the skill sets a technician requirements.

Module - A technical component part of the skill set.

Multi-craft - Maintenance person that demonstrates several skills in the maintenance areas.

Task - The smallest component of a specific technical job.

Relatively Equal - The process of making the technical elements relatively equal from pay level to pay level.

Review Board - A team that looks at the technical and active participation requirements when a technician requests a level promotion.

Plant Principles - Those guidelines developed at the plant level that gives direction to the design of the high performance work structure.

Skill Set - That amount of specific technical and active participation that equates to a level in a specific department.

Technician - Employee that is paid based on overall contribution to the organization rather that time on the job.

Traditional System - Promotion systems that are based primarily on the amount of time with an organization.

Utility Skill - A person in a traditional organization that demonstrates more than two specific job areas.

Utilization - The actual use of technical and active participation at some routine frequency.

Index

A

Able and willing 9,10
Able but unwilling 9,12, 169
Active participation 36,37,104-106
Attributes 6,9
Availability Minimum 153-155
             Maximum 156,157

B

Buckeye Cellulose 38
Building blocks 82

C

Calibration of skills 26,92-95
Career pathing/planning 180
Certification board 175,179
Communication 71
Components of high performance 26,27
Corporate support 42

D

Department Management 51,52
           (new plant) 76
Demonstration 178,179
Design elements 47
Design (Plant) 46,61-68
Design (Dept) 68-70
Distress 4
Domino effect 16,32

E

Equal 14
Electrical/instrumentation 139
Exhibit A
Traditional distribution 23
Exhibit B
Normal distribution 24
Exhibit C
Umbrella 28
Exhibit D
Relationships 84
Exhibit E
Questions 88
Exhibit F
Active Participation 107
Exhibit G
Active Participation 115
Exhibit H
Matrix operational 122
Exhibit I
Matrix fixed mech 132
Exhibit J
Matrix Modular mech 135
Exhibit K
Matrix modular/fixed 138
Exhibit L
Matrix fixed e/i 145
Exhibit M

Matrix modular e/i 146
Exhibit N
Matrix modular/fixed 148
Exhibit O
Matrix oper/maint 151
Exhibit P
Matrix operational 185
Exhibit Q
Matrix operational/2 189
Exhibit R
Career path 193

F
Facilitator 65
Fairness 14

G
Gathering information 88
Guidelines (corporate) 43

H
I
Information 86

J
K

L
Levels 82,84

M
Maintenance skills 17,123 - 125
Matrix (see exhibits)
Matrix (advantages) 190
Multi-craft 19-22
Maximum availability 155,156
Minimum availability 153,154

N
New plant
       design 73-80
O
P
Pay levels 27
       rates 159-163
Q
R
Relatively equal 101,102
Review boards 29
Rosy 74

S
Skills 149
Skill sets 26,34
Supervisor 53-58
   (new plant) 77,78

T
Task areas 96-98
Technician 59,60
Tradition 5
Training 220,29,169,170,172

Transition 157

U
Utility 21,171
Umbrella (see exhibit) 26
Unwilling and unable 9

V

W
Willamette Ind 45
Willing but unable 11

Appendix

Assoications

American Management Association (AMA)
135 W 50th St
New York, NY 10020-1201

Paper Industry Management Association
2400 East Oakton St
Arlington Heights, Il 60005

Encyclopedia of Associations
29th Edition
Gale Research Inc.
835 Penobscot Bldg
Detroit, MI 48226-4094
(contains a large listing of associations for every type of industry)

Training Resources

Development Dimensions International
1225 Washington Pike
Bridgeville, PA 15017-2838

IDCON Incorporated
7200 Falls of Neuse Rd
Suite 200
Raleigh, North Carolina
        27615-5311

Consultants for High Performance Work Structures

Matrix Systems Incorporated
Richard Allison, President
P.O. Box 1510
Cheraw, South Carolina
29520
Phone 803-537-0553

"The Business Resource Network, Inc."
John L. Sipple, President
115 Tamerlane
Peachtree City, Georgia
30269
Phone/Fax 770-486-0533

Suggested Reading

The Deming Management Method
by Mary Walton
Putnam Publishing

Leadership Secrets of Attila the Hun
Wess Roberts PHD
Warner Books

In Search of Excellence
Tom Peters
Harper Row

Paradigms - The Business of Discovering the Future
Morrow

Coaching for Improved Work Performance
Ferdinand F. Fournies
Liberty House

The 7 Habits of Highly Successful People
Steven R.Covey
Simon and Schuster

Zapp
William C. Byham, PHD
First Harmony Books

For more information on:

High Performance Work Structures

or

Ordering information for the book

Please Die - I Want A Promotion

*How to Maximize Employee
Flexibility and Contribution*

Call or Write:

**Matrix Systems Incorporated
P.O. Box 1510
Cheraw, South Carolina
29520**

Phone: 803-537-0553

To Order Copies of

Please Die I Want A Promotion

Complete the information below
Ship to: (please print)

Company Name _____
Attention   _____
Address   _____
City,State,Zip _____

Day Phone   _____

Number of copies @ 17.95 each   _____

Postage and Handling @ 3.00 per book   _____

        Total amount enclosed   _____

_____ check   _____ money order

Purchase order number _____

Make payable to: **Matrix Systems Inc.**

Send to: **Matrix Systems Inc.**
       P.O. Box 1510
       Cheraw, South Carolina 29520

       or phone 803-537-0553

Notes

Notes

Notes

Notes